For 21 years Dr James A. Sim... ...och
Cathedral in the Scottish H... ...not
only served as captain of th... ...ote
many books, some of whi... ...*and*
Laughter, topped Scottish be... ...lar
contributor to magazines an... ...papers, not only in Scotland, but also in the USA. He is also much in demand as an after-dinner speaker.

In 1992 he was appointed chaplain to the Queen in Scotland. Two years later he was elected Moderator of the General Assembly of the Church of Scotland.

Dr Simpson has long believed that in any lecture, discussion or debate a little comic relief does no harm, no matter how serious the topic may be.

By the same author

There Is a Time to...
Marriage Questions Today
Doubts Are Not Enough
Keywords of Faith
Holy Wit
Laughter Lines
The Master Mind
More Holy Wit
All About Christmas
The Laugh Shall Be First
Life, Love and Laughter
A Funny Way of Being Serious

At Our Age

Humorous and Insightful Reflections on the Ageing Process

James A. Simpson

Steve Savage
LONDON AND EDINBURGH

Steve Savage Publishers Ltd
The Old Truman Brewery
91 Brick Lane
LONDON
E1 6QL

www.savagepublishers.com

First published in Great Britain by Steve Savage Publishers Ltd 2010

ISBN: 978-1-904246-34-3

Typeset by Steve Savage Publishers Ltd
Printed and bound by SRP Ltd, Exeter

Contents

Dedicated to

Helen

my wife and best friend

for fifty years

Introduction

I'm not getting deafer, but people speak lower
They're walking faster, not me getting slower.

Take one good breath while still in bed
One cautious stretch from toe to head
If nothing hurts you must be dead.

Grant me the senility to forget the people I never liked anyway
The good fortune to run into the ones I do
And the eyesight to tell the difference.

Most books and articles on the subject of ageing have been written by men and women in their late fifties or early sixties, few in their late seventies and eighties. The distinguished Roman lawyer Cicero, in a famous essay entitled *De Senectute*, (Of Old Age), written when he was 62, sought to convince his readers that advancing years will pour out their rewards as from a horn of plenty. He speaks of old men as being 'reasonable and not churlish'. He says, 'The writing of this essay has been so delightful that it has not only wiped away all the disagreeables of old age, but has even made it luxurious and delightful too.' Aristotle viewed old age very differently. He savagely depicted old people as selfish, unenthusiastic, mean, hard and cynical. I believe the truth is somewhere in between. In this book I want to look not only at some of the delights of growing older, but also at what Lord Byron called 'the woes that wait on age.'

The serene face and outlook of an 89-year-old lady greatly impressed me. When asked what her secret was, she replied,

'Well, when I was sixty-five, I looked over my shoulder and saw old age catching up on me. So I just stood aside and let it pass.' Believing as I do that the most entrancing words in any language are 'Once upon a time...', this book, like many of my previous books, is full of stories, stories which, like the one I have just shared, not only gave me food for thought, but caused me to laugh. I hope the stories will also cause the readers to stop, think and chuckle. We get better wrinkles from laughing than frowning.

The royalties from this book will once again go to supporting Cystic Fibrosis research and people like my much-loved grand-daughter Sally who suffers from this very debilitating disease.

My thanks are due to two friends – to Margaret Thomson of Perth for proof-reading the manuscript – and to Stuart Wallace of Eaglesham for sketching the cartoon for the cover.

Living Longer than Expected

'None are so old as those who have outlived enthusiasm.'
Henry Thoreau

An old lady who went to her doctor to see if anything might be done about her very sore knee, began by saying, 'Doctor, I know you will probably say it is old age.' Before she could say any more the doctor interrupted her: 'I am not going to say that at all. It is diminishing youth.' Diminishing youth is an age-old problem about which many of us are becoming increasingly familiar. The following are I believe some of its commonest indications or symptoms.

When we no longer stoop to pick up any coin less than 10p in value.

When the end of a man's tie does not come anywhere near the top of his trousers.

When we prefix words with 'wee'. 'I will just have a wee lie down, or take a wee seat, or fix myself a wee drink.'

When people phone you at 9 a.m. and ask, 'Did I wake you?'

When we pick up our phone when the phone rings on television.

When we have a party and our neighbours don't even notice.

When there are many crossed-off names in our address book.

When we are cautioned to slow down by the doctor instead of the police.

When it becomes an achievement to do thoughtfully, step by step, what we once did instinctively.

When we are on first-name terms with our chemist.

When more and more of our purchases are 'For fast-acting relief'.

When our medicine cabinet is better stocked than our drinks cabinet.

When 'a girl' is an elderly woman of our own age.

When we spend more time looking for things than we spend using them when we find them.

When we recall things that never actually happened, and are praised for things we never did.

When we think other people are not having the fun we had.

When the shop assistant picks out the appropriate coins from our handful of change.

When we still try to get electrical gadgets repaired when they go wrong.

When we and our teeth don't sleep together.

When we can sing while cleaning our teeth!

When it takes two tries to get up from the couch.

When after painting the town red we have to take a long rest before applying the second coat.

When our family worry if we are dead when we are simply having a nap.

When getting lucky means we find our car in the parking lot.

When we listen to jokes and catch everything but the punch-line.

When on hearing disco music we want to clap our hands – over our ears!

It is a strange feeling being in your mid-seventies. I don't feel seventy-six, but then what does seventy-six feel like? Advancing years have been creeping up on me and many of my friends for some time. Funerals increasingly fill my diary. Though one might think that saying goodbye to dear friends might get easier over time, it is anything but.

These days I am often taken aback by the person I view each morning in the mirror, a man who looks more and more like my father. I am also slowly beginning to realise that in our family circle there has been a 'role reversal'. My children, now all middle-aged, keep urging me to 'go more carefully', not to shovel snow, not to clean gutters.

I have long been fascinated by the way we use different verbs in counting major birthdays – We turn 30, push 40, reach 50, make it to 60 and hit 75. Having passed 75, I would echo the sentiments of the old man who said, 'Forget ageing. If your head is still well above the ground and you are still looking at the green side of the turf, then it is a good day.' I personally am prepared to put up with a few health problems and other inconveniences in order to go on enjoying, for hopefully at least a few more years, a life that up to now has been a wonderful experience.

Coming from a family with mixed fortunes regarding life-span, I am extremely fortunate to have been blessed with years beyond not only the Biblical allotted span but what I had any right to expect. My mother died when I was a teenager. My brother died of heart problems in his 40s. I on the other hand with the help of a couple of 'stents' and blood pressure pills, and a wonderful wife who was formerly a nurse, have been rewarded with seventy-six good and healthy years. Whatever the future holds, the bargain so far has been good.

One of the most far reaching developments of the 20th century was that for the first time in recorded history, thanks to improved working conditions, better housing, sanitation and nutrition, medical advances and life-threatening conditions becoming treatable, it became normal in the Western world to grow old. Previously living to a ripe old age was the experience of only a small minority of people. A burial ground in Dundee with many very old tombstones reveals that over half the population in the 18th century were dead before they were 30. At the start of the 19th century, life expectancy rose to 40. Today it is 76 for men, and almost ten years more for women. Today the over-85s are statistically the fastest growing age-group.

Old age is now the longest season in human life, a period covering from 65 to 110. In no other period of life do we find so many years lumped into one category. Up to the age of 30 – the period covering childhood, adolescence and young adulthood – people are deemed young. From 30–60 they are commonly regarded as middle-aged. From then on people are simply classified as old, even though there are definite characteristics that distinguish them as belonging in younger-older, middle-older and older-older categories.

What changes there have been in the life-style of the elderly during the past hundred years. At the beginning of the 20th century the majority of women over 70 were bespectacled, sock-knitting and white-haired. Many of them seemed resigned to a slow slippered twilight. They wore dark clothing which sometimes had a mothball smell, and seldom ventured far from home. Today they have life-styles their parents would have found unimaginable. Living independent lives, they wear far brighter and more fashionable clothes. They surf the net and regularly travel abroad. When one such eighty-year-old woman was congratulated on being so spry for a woman of her age, she retorted sharply, 'I will have you know that I am not a woman of my age!'

Things I Used to Do

One of the first signs of old age is when you hear 'snap, crackle, pop' in the morning and it is not your cereal.

There are many things I used to do, but don't do any more –

I no longer wind up my watch.

I no longer carry a fountain pen.

I no longer use carbon paper.

I no longer wear darned socks.

I no longer use a record player to listen to music.

I no longer carry my golf clubs, or play more than 18 holes in one day.

I no longer dream of becoming a scratch golfer. I now realise that is not going to happen.

I no longer worry about birth control. My concern now is more girth control.

I no longer run to catch a bus or train.

I no longer buy patterned carpets.

I can no longer hum modern pop music.

I don't whisper any more, perhaps because I don't have as many secrets as I used to.

I no longer go up or down the stairs two at a time.

I no longer lie on the floor in front of the television, simply because it is now so much harder to get up.

BUT

Inside I still think young.

I rejoice that my enthusiasm for life is undiminished, and my capacity for enjoyment is far from exhausted.

I still have the urge when it snows to throw snowballs.

I have retained my competitive spirit, but no longer to the stage of biting my nails.

I still cherish dreams I would love to make come true.

I now feel more intensely and compliment people more than I used to.

I continue to laugh at my own foibles and foolishness.

I rejoice that I am slower to judge, quicker to understand and more ready to forgive.

I am now more aware of how easily I could have made a shipwreck of my own life.

I am less concerned about making an impression.

I still try to demonstrate gratitude in thoughtful ways.

I now feel sorry for people who live in the past. I know it was cheaper then, but if you keep looking in the rear-view mirror you will soon have a stiff neck.

I don't worry the same about making a fool of myself by the expression in public of an honest thought.

❧

My hope is that I will grow old as graciously as a 90-year-old friend. Though not physically well, his mind and spirit are as alert as ever. Secure in his faith, he seldom complains about the inevitable physical problems of diminishing youth. Another octogenarian, equally uncomplaining, wrote

> *There is nothing the matter with me,*
> *I'm as healthy as I can be.*
> *I have arthritis in both my knees*
> *And when I talk, I talk with a wheeze.*
> *My pulse is weak, and my blood is thin*
> *But I'm awfully well for the shape I am in.*

Arch supports I have for my feet
Or I wouldn't be able to be on the street.
Sleep is denied me night after night
But every morning I find I'm all right.
The moral is this as my tale I unfold
That for you and me who are growing old,
It is better to say, 'I'm fine' with a grin
Than to let folks know the shape I am in.

The A–Z of Old Age

Live well and die young at as old an age as possible.

Old age is a state which all wish to attain, and at which we grumble when attained.

When Francis Bacon said in commendation of old age, 'Just as old wood is best to burn, old wine to drink, so old age is the best period of our lives,' he was, I believe, overstating the case. Diminishing youth has drawbacks. I sympathise with the retired gentleman who said, 'Trying to stay healthy is just about killing me. Jogging has ruined my knees. Lifting weights has strained my back. Swimming has given me sinusitis.' I recently read an A–Z of medical problems associated with diminishing youth. Let me share just a few. A is for Arthritis; B is for Bad Back; C is for Chest pains; D is for Dental Decay. E is for Eyesight that is failing; F is for Fluid retention; G is for Gas and other gastrointestinal glitches; H is for Hysterectomy. (The mention of hysterectomy reminds me of a woman who was very nervous about her forthcoming operation. Her anxiety was increased when the night before the operation, a young nurse asked her, 'Have you had a hysterectomy before?') I is for Itches; J is for Joints that are failing to flex, ... R is for Reflux – one meal becomes two! ... But that is more than enough of this medical alphabet.

Had the alphabet been male-oriented, B could well have stood for baldness. Someone said that one of the few advantages of being bald is that you can 'hear' snowflakes! Pam Ayres had bald people in mind when she wrote about men who in their youth were so 'extravagantly maned' that in the cinema those who sat behind them used to 'rant as they tried to see Cary Grant.' She finished her very humorous poem telling how these same men are now willing to 'offer free to a loving home, one redundant brush and comb.'

❧

Somerset Maugham, who suffered from a stutter, was invited to address a prestigious gathering on his eightieth birthday. After dinner he rose, thanked his hosts, took a sip from a glass of water and began, 'Old age has many benefits...' There then followed a long and painful silence. He tried sipping some more water. He shuffled his notes, trying several times to speak, but finally sat down. Like those present that night, I would have loved to have known what he intended to say about the benefits and pleasures of old age, for they are real. Though there is a beauty about the morning and a radiance about noon, there is also something very attractive about drawing the curtains, turning on the light and enjoying the tranquillity of evening. I think of the boiled down wisdom which often comes through years of seeing and touching, succeeding and failing, caring and sacrificing, sleepless nights and memories of enriching experiences. Another major advantage which older people have over younger people is that having once been young and now being old, they know both ages. Young people on the other hand can only guess what it is like to be old.

❧

Some of the other compensations of diminishing youth are more humorous. A 100-year-old said, 'There is very little peer pressure now.' Another old lady spoke of the delight of whirling past in an airport buggie those on the long trek to the departure gate. In a hostage situation the elderly are more likely to be among those released first. Getting a free bus pass and free medicines, and no longer being able to read the bathroom scales, are additional bonuses.

❦

People often have to get old before anyone says they are looking young. When a friend said recently, 'You look wonderful,' I suspect what he really meant was, 'For someone as old as you are, you don't look bad.' I still feel young, but there is no denying that in your mid-70s you do slow down. You don't have the same energy. You crank yourself down and up to pick up a spoon or pen that has fallen. I am now at the stage when everything is beginning to click – elbows, knees, neck, back. But fortunately I am not yet at the stage of the old man who when asked if he felt his age, replied, 'No, in fact I don't feel anything until noon.' In similar vein I heard of an elderly man who said to his neighbour, 'The happy hour – that for me is now the afternoon nap.' Another elderly gentleman when asked how old he was, paused before saying, 'Well, let us just put it this way. When I was a boy the Dead Sea was just sick.'

❦

Whereas for old-timers the years seem to flash past, for the young a year is a very long time. Many of us will recall how when we were less than fifteen we tended to think in fractions. We told those who asked our age, how we were ten and a half, or nine and three-quarters. One little lad, when asked his age, proudly said, 'I'm half past four.' This burning desire to be older did not however last long. The older we became the more we came to see that many of the signs of getting older are not attractive. I have already mentioned a number of them. Others include our reaction time slowing up, our hands shaking, our stride shortening, our legs becoming less shapely, our emotions more fragile. Our knees buckle, but our belt won't. Our back goes out more than we do. The little old lady we now help across the road is our wife. When we sink our teeth into a Pavlova, they sometimes stay there. I smiled when a friend of mine, who is considerably more corpulent than I am, claimed that the ageing process had made his wife's arms shorter. He explained that when they had got married she could put her arms right round him!

❦

I wonder if like me you sometimes get the feeling nature is conspiring against you for the financial benefit of chiropractors, chemists, hearing aid manufacturers and dentists. The price of dentistry has become such that the phrase 'putting your money where your mouth is' has taken on a whole new meaning.

Loss of hearing is a major loss. I would not like at my age to be confronted with the Faustian dilemma of either losing my sight or hearing. It would be a fearfully difficult choice. I would not want to be cut off from the beauty of the world around us, or the world of conversation and music.

I could not but smile recently when I heard about an 85-year-old man who told his doctor that he was beginning to slow down sexually. When the doctor asked when he began to notice this, he said, 'Last night, and again this morning!'

Another elderly gentleman, who had been plagued with serious hearing problems for a number of years, was finally fitted with the very latest hearing aid. A month later he returned for a final check-up. After some tests, the specialist informed him that thanks to the new hearing aid, his hearing was now well above average. The man thanked the doctor profusely. 'You are welcome,' said the doctor. 'Your family must really be pleased you can hear again.' 'Oh, I have not told them yet. I just sit around and listen to the conversations I used to miss.' 'Really?' said the specialist. 'Is it because you are having difficulty accepting that your hearing is so improved, or because you question whether the improvement will last?' 'No, that is not the reason at all. Having heard what they are saying about me, I have already changed my will three times.'

I have heard women bitterly complain that the only thing they have gained by becoming older is weight, and that whereas they used to say, 'The night is young', now they can barely keep their eyes open after the 10 o'clock News.

Grandfather and I

Grandparents have the pleasure of seeing the third edition of their autobiographies, revised and often improved!

Few books have jolted me more than the children's picture book *Grandfather and I.* 'Grandfather and I are going for a walk. It will be a slow walk because grandfather and I never hurry. We walk along and stop and look, just as long as we like. Other people we know are always in a hurry. Mothers hurry. They walk in a hurry and talk in a hurry, and they always want you to hurry. But grandfather and I never hurry. We walk along and stop and look just as long as we like. Fathers hurry. They hurry off to work and they hurry home again. They hurry when they kiss you and when they take you for a ride. When grandfather and I get home we sit in a chair and rock and rock, and sing a little and talk a little, until somebody tells us to hurry.' The scary thing is that far too often that is painfully true.

The book reminded me of the central character in one of Aldous Huxley's short stories. Oscar gives generously of his time, money and energy to worthy causes. Oscar is a very busy man, so busy that his family life turns sour. It seems to have been similar with the writer of the Old Testament book 'The Song of Solomon'. He laments, 'They made me keeper of the vineyards; but my own vineyard I have not kept.' Many of the big names in the Old Testament did not rate highly as parents. Isaac made the elementary mistake of having favourites, preferring Esau to Jacob. Jacob made the same mistake with Joseph and in doing so put the rest of the family's back up. Eli the elderly priest helped the boy

Samuel on the road to righteousness, but could not control his own sons. And when Samuel grew up and became busy with the affairs of God, it is recorded that his sons 'were intent on their own profit; they took bribes and perverted the course of justice.' 'Behold you are old,' the elders say to Samuel, 'and your sons do not follow in your footsteps.' The same could have been said to David about his son Absalom.

❦

A teenager said of his father, 'Dad always used to say, "We will see." I soon learned that what he really meant was "No."' Unfortunately some parents are so busy at their work, or so involved with hobbies or sports in which they have a special interest – so busy in these vineyards that they neglect the vineyards of home and family in which life's most significant values should take root and grow. Many head teachers believe that family breakdown, or neglect, is an even greater threat to pupils' well-being than drugs or alcohol. This being so, grandparents who make time to be with their grandchildren and play with them and listen to them are rendering immense service. 'Grandparents,' said one little girl, 'fill the gap that mothers and fathers often leave out.' That is true in many families. Today grandparents are much more than a tuck shop, a fount of goodies and presents, or a safety shield against an angry Mum. They are the biggest providers of child care in Britain. Thirteen million grandparents currently care for their children's children on a regular basis. By showing them caring love and making time to listen to them, they are giving them a sense of security, they are helping build young lives that will be reasonably resistant to life's storms.

Grandparents and Grandchildren

Grandchildren are the wonderful reward
for not killing your teenagers!

Having grandchildren is one of the solid pleasures of old age. One grand-daughter wrote of her double-decker mother, 'I would turn the corner on my way home from school and there she would be waving from the dining room window. She was what a grandmother ought to be – soft and warm, so that as I wrapped my arms round her neck, I sank in as into a ball of angora yarn.' I worry about middle-aged women who go on starvation diets so that they can squeeze into size 8 mod fashions. What kind of grandmothers are they going to be?

❧

The Greek actress Melina Mercouri tells in her autobiography that the first man she loved was Spiros. He was extremely handsome. She adored his embrace. He was strong and tall. He had a passion for her. It made her childhood a very happy one. Spiros was her grandfather, a mayor of Athens for 30 years!

❧

Almost every generation revolts against its parents and makes friends with its grandparents. I vividly recall back in the 1940s being sent to the ice-cream shop with a glass jug to get so many dollops of ice-cream for visitors who were coming for lunch. Years later I heard a delightful story about a little boy in Largs who was sent one cold Saturday morning on a similar errand to Nardini's, Largs' famous ice-cream shop. Friends were coming for lunch. Having got the glass jug filled with the necessary amount of ice-cream, he set off home. On the way he met some of his pals playing football in the street, as boys regularly did in the 1940s. It being very cold, he thought it would not harm the ice-cream if he joined them for a few minutes. Putting the jug with the ice-cream on a nearby garden wall, he joined in the game. Unfortunately the ball hit the jug and it fell to the pavement breaking into a thousand pieces. There was total silence, until one wee lad said, 'Have you not got a grannie you could go to?' Grandma was the only person who might possibly rescue him from the terrible mess he was in.

❧

There is a special bond between grandchildren and grandparents. Many have spoken of a feeling of renewal and purpose in their lives when a grandchild is born. Having more time, they enjoy getting close to their grandchildren. A Dr Campbell tells of a wealthy American who had three married daughters. He and his wife were saddened, however, that they had no grandchildren. One day when they were all visiting with their husbands, the father said at the dinner table that he had something important to tell the family. 'You have probably guessed that your Mum and I miss having grandchildren. Well, we have talked it over. I have had a good year financially, so we have decided to give a million dollars to the couple who give us our first grandchild.' Then he bowed his head to say grace. When he finished, only his wife and himself were at the table.

❧

An American grandmother was hurriedly called from Washington to help with an emergency at her daughter's home in Ontario. Her car was stopped at the Canadian border for the usual Customs examination. When the officer asked if she had anything to declare, she replied, 'No, I have only come to spend a few days with my grandchildren.' With a disbelieving look, he replied, 'What kind of grandmother are you – coming all that way and you have nothing for the grandkids?'

❧

When his tenth grandchild was born, the baby's grandfather rushed to the hospital with his camcorder. As he proudly taped his new grand-daughter, the nurse who had come into the room asked him, 'Is this your first grandchild?' 'No,' he replied, 'it is my first camcorder.'

❧

Grandchildren keep you young, but it is also true that after spending time with them you feel your age. How numerous are the stories recalling the most unexpected things grandchildren say. A grandmother tells how while out walking with her four-year-old grand-daughter, they came across a flattened hedgehog on the road. Glancing at the squashed creature, the wee lass shook her head and said, 'Well Grandma, he certainly did not hold his mummy's hand, did he?'

❧

A friend Anne Pollock was baking one day with her two-year-old grand-daughter. At one stage of their conversation, Anne asked her if she knew her own name. Slightly surprised by the question the wee girl replied, 'Jessica.' 'Oh I know that,' said Anne, 'but what is your other name?' Jessica hesitated before saying, 'Lovely wee girl.' So many people had said to her, 'You are a lovely wee girl,' that she obviously thought this was her second name.

Another grandmother asked her grand-daughter what sounds animals make. She had no difficulty giving the correct answers to the sounds that horses, sheep and cows make, but when asked the sound a mouse makes, to the grandmother's surprise, the obviously computer literate child replied, 'Click, Click.'

Though money does not necessarily buy parents and grandparents happiness, it does in our later years, keep us in touch with our children and grandchildren! An eight-year-old boy wrote, 'Grandparents are so old that they should not play hard or run. But it is good if they drive us to the shops and give us money.'

A Grandpa was relaxing with his young grandson seated on the arm of his chair. Looking down at his grandfather he said lovingly, 'Grandpa, your hair is like the waves.' Then after a short pause he continued, 'And the tide has gone out.'

A schoolgirl grand-daughter wrote to her grandmother in hospital, 'Dear Gran, Mummy told me you were in hospital for tests. I hope you get an A.'

One day when Grannie was baby-sitting for her grand-daughter, the little girl was playing with her family of dolls. Finally she tucked them in her pram and turned to her Grannie with a worried expression. 'I don't know how I am going to manage all these children. I am expecting again this Christmas.'

A Grandpa and his teenage grand-daughter were arguing whether pop stars should be deemed celebrities. 'But Grandpa,' said his grand-daughter, 'Elvis Presley is one of the most famous people in the world.' 'Elvis Presley. He is not famous,' retorted Grandpa. 'That bloke who invented penicillin...what is his name? He is famous.'

When John's grandfather asked him what position he played in the school football team, John said he was not sure, but he thought he had heard his teacher refer to him as the team's main drawback.

Hearing that the clocks were to go back at the weekend, a little girl said to her grandmother, 'At least we still have our watches.'

Addressing his grandchildren, a very elderly man said, 'I have never drunk alcohol, I have never smoked, never been to bed after 10 p.m., and never eaten too much. And you know what? Tomorrow I celebrate my 100th birthday.' After a short pause one of his great-grandsons said, 'Grandpa, how are you going to celebrate?'

While his wife was washing the supper dishes, Grandpa offered to bath his four grandsons, including the three-year-old twins. After tidying up the bathroom, he emerged to find three shining faces and one that was still dirty. The clean twin ran to his grandma and gleefully announced: 'Grandpa gave me two baths.'

'If you are happy,' said one small boy to his grandfather, 'why don't you tell your face?'

A nine-year-old grandson had difficulty believing that his grandfather could possibly have enjoyed life back in the Dark Ages when there were no mobile phones or iPods or colour television. 'You know, Grandpa, now when I think of you as a little boy I will always think of you in black and white.'

On a lengthy car journey John's grand-daughter kept asking, 'Are we nearly there?' When he told her that it would be dark before they reached their destination, the wee lass asked, 'Grandpa, is it nearly dark?'

A Welsh grandmother tells how her four-year-old grandson always managed to answer the phone before anyone else. One day she decided to see if he recognised her voice. After he answered, she said, 'Hello Daniel, who am I?' This was followed by a short silence, then a shout, 'Mum, Nanny's on the phone and she does not know who she is.'

My wife was thrilled recently when she received a card from two of our grand-daughters with the lovely message, 'You are never too old to be young at heart.'

The neighbour of a man whose grandchildren were visiting one Christmas, said to him, 'I bet you are looking forward to having a child-free house once again.' 'Yes,' he said, 'and an apple that has not got teeth marks in it.'

A Mrs Badger tells how they took their grandson to Sea World in Florida. For some reason unknown to them he absolutely refused to watch the show featuring Shamu the killer whale. No amount of discussion could get him to change his mind. Not until they got home did they discover the reason for his reluctance. An aunt had told him how exciting the show would be because 'they choose children from the audience to feed Shamu.'

A Mr Robinson tells how he was enjoying a game of cricket on the lawn with his four-year-old grandson and his son-in-law. After a while his daughter came out and asked if she could join in. The wee lad, though obviously not very enthusiastic, finally agreed. 'All right Mummy', he said, 'you stand there and be the vampire.'

One grandmother described her grandchildren as her 'miniatures' because 'the miniature back is turned, they are up to mischief!'

When a mother was asked if she had made the long trip to Australia to visit her son and his new wife who were expecting their first baby. 'No, I'm waiting until the baby arrives. You see I have a theory that grandmas are more welcome than mothers-in-law.'

Doing, Getting, Being

'To grow old is to pass from passion to compassion.'
Camus

When Penelope Keith was once asked whether there was any one character in fiction with whom she identified, she replied, 'It changes as you get older. I used to weep for Romeo and Juliet. Now that I am older, I think, their poor parents.' Our thinking on many subjects does change with the passing years. The ageing process can help us sort out our priorities. We come to see more clearly what things in life matter a great deal and what don't matter all that much.

❧

Years ago many of us probably read some of Alistair Maclean's best-sellers or watched films based on his novels, like *The Guns of Navarone*. What is not commonly known is that Alistair Maclean's father was for many years the minister of Daviot Church, the little church you pass as you climb the hill nearing Inverness on the A9. In one of his books, *High Country*, Alistair Maclean Sr sums up how his thinking changed with the passing years. He writes, 'When we are young we want to *do* things. When the middle years come we want to *get* things. But when the westward years appear, we want to *be* things.' Though that generalisation might not be sufficiently universal to satisfy some philosophers, there is a great deal of food for thought in it.

Most young people are full of vitality and energy. They don't want to stop during their waking hours. They want to know in the morning what they are going to do in the afternoon.

At bedtime they want to know what they are going to do the following day. Their constant question is, 'What are we going to do next?' As they approach adolescence, the things young people want to do change but still their prime concern is doing things.

When the middle years come the desire to do things is often surpassed by the desire to get things.

Because in our Western culture things possessed have become the symbol of success and the index of superiority, many are tempted to assume that the getting mode of existence is in fact the natural, normal way of life, that the more we have the happier we shall be, that the fullest enrichment of our lives can come only from an abundance of possessions. Using brain-washing techniques our parents never dreamed of, advertisers seek to get us to consume more and more. I sometimes think their avowed aim is to keep us in a perpetual state of discontent. 'To attain, to advance, to acquire until death do us part.' I can think of many proud people who pass that sentence on themselves in their middle years.

'When we are young we want to *do* things, when the middle years come we want to *get* things, but when the westward years appear we want to *be* things' – to be more fully human, alive to truth and beauty and the needs of others, a friend to many. One of the advantages of advancing years is a change in perspective. Desires expand and change with living. 'Oh,' but some will say, 'I shall always want success.' Perhaps, but what they count success at 25 they may not count success at 65. Nancy Astor on her 80th birthday observed that she used to dread getting older because she thought she would not be able to do all the things she wanted to do – but now that she was older she found she did not want to do many of them anyway. The playwright Dennis Potter also underwent a process of re-evaluation. In an interview he gave two weeks before he died of cancer, he said that some things were now more trivial than they had ever been, and others more important than they ever were. It was no different with Malcolm Muggeridge, the former editor of *Punch*. He told how, 'When I embarked on the voyage of life, I worried about having a cabin with a port-hole, whether I would be asked to sit at the captain's table, who were the most attractive and important passengers. I now see how unimportant all such considerations are... The passion to accumulate possessions, to be noticed and deemed important, is now too evidently absurd to be entertained.'

It is a pity that many who expend so much time and nervous energy in the struggle to get to the next rung of the ladder, seldom stop and ask where the ladder is leading. The problem with the craving for wealth and possessions, celebrity status and power, is that acquiring these things often requires the sacrifice of health, family life, friends and sometimes self-respect. How relevant is Jesus' question, 'What do people gain if they win the whole world at the cost of their true self?' The American novelist Anna Quindlen, in an address she gave to college graduates, quoted some words of her father: 'If you win the rat race, you are still a rat.' She pled with the graduating students to diminish the instincts that centre on possession, not to succumb to the manic pursuit of the next promotion, the bigger pay cheque and a larger house.

The ageing process can bring a wisdom, a new value system, a grace and a less combative stance, born of a longer-range view of life. In our saner moments, most of us know that we are essentially human beings, not human getters. The problem is that in the middle years, we are seldom sane. Often it is not until well on in life that people realise that what we are is of greater significance than what we own, that life's most precious things, the ability to love and laugh, the opportunity to brighten the lives of those with whom we come into contact, to be of use, to create beauty and harmony, to enjoy the wonder of the natural world, are not dependent on great wealth or fame. One old Highlander expressed it well – 'The land may be the laird's, but the landscape is mine.' When in our later years our children and grandchildren want to be with us, that is another priceless bonus.

Our Physical and Mental Ages

If only youth knew. If only age could.

'Every woman is only twenty years old
in one corner of her heart'
Alexandre Dumas

A doctor who had studied in Scotland spent all his working life in a practice in England. He and his wife decided for his 60th birthday to return for a weekend to the town in which he had been brought up and educated. On the drive north he developed the most awful toothache. Certain that, unless attended to, it would ruin their weekend, he inquired at the hotel reception desk if there might be a dentist in the town who would be willing to see him. Within a few minutes the receptionist phoned their room to say that there was a dentist who was willing to see him at five o'clock. Arriving at the surgery he noticed, written on the brass plate at the door, Michael Brown BDS. That is strange, he thought, there was a Michael Brown in my class at school. I wonder if it is the same person. But when taken through to the surgery and introduced to the dentist, a man with pure white hair, wrinkled skin and great bags under his eyes, he thought it could not possibly be the same person. He was sure the dentist was at least ten years older than him. While waiting for the pain-killing injection to work, he inquired whether the dentist was native to the area. When informed that he was, the doctor asked when he had been at secondary school. 'Oh I was there from sixty to sixty-five.' 'That is strange,' said the doctor, 'I was there at exactly the same time.' On hearing this, the dentist asked, 'What did you teach?'

Most of us tend to think of ourselves as being fifteen years younger than we actually are. It is hard mentally to accept that we are becoming old. I still think of myself as looking the way I did before I retired. At a recent college reunion I met an old university class-mate whom I had not seen for 45 years. We had studied together at Glasgow University. He had aged so much that he did not recognise me! I got to thinking about it the following morning. As I was doing so, I glanced at my own reflection in our modern bathroom mirror. Then I realised they just don't make good mirrors any more! I relate to the answer which Bruce Bliven, a former editor, gave when asked what it was like to be an old man: 'I don't feel like an old man. I feel like a young man with some physical things the matter with him.' In Scotland, Probus Clubs for retired professional and business men have become very popular. With tongue in cheek someone suggested that the letters of PROBUS stand for 'Prostate Removed, Other Bits Under Suspicion!'

In some respects our ageing bodies are like old cars. Bits and pieces begin to go wrong. In a talk which a doctor gave about healthy living, he elaborated on the similarities between the human body and the car. He stressed the importance of putting the right fuel into the system for the best performance, and the need to look after the bodywork... and so on. When at the end of his talk he invited questions and comments, one man, who had a lively sense of humour, said, 'Doctor, if this body of mine was a car, this would be the time I would be thinking of trading it in for a new model. The body-work has so many bumps and scratches. The outside paint is much duller. The headlights are out of focus. My traction is not as graceful as it once was. It also takes me much longer to get up to a reasonable speed. The fuel burns less efficiently. And every time I sneeze, cough or splutter, my radiator leaks or my exhaust backfires.'

Writing about ageing, Thomas Jefferson said in a letter to John Adams, 'Our machines have now been running for almost eighty years, and we must expect that, worn as they are, here a pivot, there a wheel, now a pinion, next a spring will be giving way, and however we may tinker with them for a while, all will at length surcease motion.' The revelation that the number of centenarians and 110-year-olds is set to increase dramatically – whether as a result of drinking eight glasses of water a day (not seven and not nine) or the result of genetic engineering, or spending many sweaty hours in a gym, or as a result of new drugs or the implanting of electronic systems into the body – is not necessarily good news. Even if I was equipped at a hundred with a turbo-charged wheel-chair, there would be the problem of remembering where I was supposed to be going.

Larger Horizons

'Take it easy' is not the high wisdom for living.
Idleness is leisure gone to seed.
Those who love deeply never grow old.

We cannot help becoming older, but we can all help getting old. The fact that we blow out more candles in the cake with every passing year does not necessarily mean that we are growing wiser. Our houses may have grown in size, our cars in horsepower, our estates in net worth – but what of ourselves? Many are so wrapped up in the siren song of their own life, so preoccupied with career, salary and status, the mortgage, and bodily changes such as wrinkles, weight increase and a sagging bottom, that they seldom step back and ask, 'Is this all? Or is something missing?' Growing older helps some people get more in touch with their insides. The realisation slowly dawns that all-important is learning how to give out love and let it come in to our lives. It is when we enter sympathetically and imaginatively into other lives, and make time to provide for others some happiness, help and comfort, that our own life becomes far more meaningful. Every act of genuine involvement encourages the growth of our identity beyond the Me to the We, intertwining us with other selves, until the thread of each life is no longer a single strand, but part of the fabric of humankind. Focussing solely on being number one, regardless of the well-being of others, leads to loneliness, isolation and depression.

A life that has no meaning beyond its own narrow horizons grows emptier and emptier. It is a hollow existence. With no interest left but self-interest there is ultimately no interest left at all. A doctor recalls a woman who was convinced her husband was being imposed upon. She regularly warned him that he should not allow others to put so many responsibilities on his shoulders. Gradually he came to believe she was right, that he was a fool to be involved in so much voluntary work. Then in a kind of mutual concern, he began to beg his wife not to tax herself in doing so much entertaining. They finally nursed and babied each other into not letting anyone or any organisation make demands on them. Their lives became more and more self-centred. What they discovered, however, was that their growing apathy and self-centred outlook robbed them of much of the joy of living.

There is no doubt that in the book of life the most difficult chapter to write is the last. A particular peril of retirement is the slump, dropping into a couch-potato armchair of physical and mental neglect. I think of a retired man who each night stays up and watches the late-night movie. He has no schedule, no demands, no involvement. Each day passes imperceptibly into the next. He feels no contrast between feeling tired and feeling relaxed. He has lost the sense of what it is like to look forward to a day off. He is preoccupied with his aches and pains. In this connection I smiled when I heard of how one afternoon a retired husband who was watching television, said to his wife, 'Jean, I never want to live in a vegetative state, dependent on some machine. If that ever happens, just pull the plug.' On hearing this she got up and unplugged the television!

❧

If our minds become dull the world will be drab. But if our minds continue to grow, retirement can be exciting. The more I observe retired people, the more convinced I become they are in a sense like plants – some go to seed, others to pot, but others blossom. Even if I could afford to retire abroad to some sunny clime and live on the basis of accumulated capital, I would have no desire to do so. Making an art form of idleness holds no attraction for me. The people I know who have done that are among the most boring and unhappy people in the world.

Just after I retired I was invited to speak at the St Andrews Day dinner in Jakarta. From there my wife and I went on to Bali for a holiday. A week on that peaceful sun-drenched island, after several speaking engagements in Indonesia, was a delight, just relaxing, reading and swimming. In the hotel, as well as tourists like ourselves, there were a few Germans, who had obviously visited the island and had decided to retire there, renting a cottage in the hotel grounds. One of them, a man whom I imagined was in his seventies, had perfected the art of getting a tan. It was fascinating to watch him each day go through the ritual of putting on sun cream at regular intervals. At the crack of dawn he was on the beach, putting down his towels on the most coveted lounger, one so positioned that with minimal effort he could move from being in the sun to being in the shade. I never once saw him read a newspaper or book. He just sunned himself, smoked his cigarettes, and watched the passers by. Now it could have been that before retiring he had led a very busy life. I don't know, but what I do know is that for me that kind of life-style, month after month, would be like basking in the sun in a cemetery. I want to continue to grow, to do more than ward off decay.

❧

An 89-year-old American Joe Connon said, 'Some men retire from business at sixty, build a house in California and thereafter do nothing but sit on the front porch and listen to their arteries hardening. Even worse is joining a year-round seashore colony, where most of the men and some of the women become golf-cranks, while others become shopping, bridge and auction-sale cranks.' A friend tells of once spending a weekend at such a seashore cottage. His host and hostess were cranks of this kind. His bedroom was next to theirs. 'I hardly got a wink of sleep, for all night long the golf-crank husband kept yelling out in his dreams, "Fore!" and instantly his auction-crank wife would yell, "Four and a half!"'

❧

The love, social contacts, interests and the feeling of personal significance that we need before we retire do not diminish after we are 60 or 65. My wife and I have been fortunate in that since retiring we have kept many old friends, and are still making new ones. Our lives continue to be enriched by interactive involvement with them, by sharing not only cups of coffee, but thoughts and feelings, joys and sorrows. The support, love and caring concern that we receive from close friends and kindly neighbours, who we know are watching out for us, are an immense bonus. We also need new outlets for our energies. William James, the distinguished professor of psychology at Harvard, was forever suggesting to his friends that they try something new, that they break the crust of habit. Voluntary work in a children's hospice, the local church and nearby prison has provided my wife with social contacts, a sense of feeling useful and fixed dates in the weekly calendar. I am glad that since retiring I have been able to help out in churches without a minister, and that I have been under obligation to write for several church magazines at home and abroad, for a golf magazine and occasionally for newspapers. For me, writing is a creative hobby. It is certainly not a chore. When I go into my study and shut the door and sit down at my computer, I am blissfully content.

I am also privileged to be invited to conduct worship, speak at golf and other dinners, and address various church, community and charitable groups. My life would be the poorer without such challenges. Others have very different hobbies in which they can lose themselves. I think of a gifted Glasgow businessman who produces concerts and musicals for local primary schools. I think of friends who have taken up wood-carving. I think of a former language teacher who on retiring studied a new language every year, presenting himself for the 'Higher' grade exam in it. The last time I spoke to Mr Jack he had ten language Highers. I think of a medical doctor who since retiring to Dornoch has written two books about the Glasgow trams. I think of other retired doctors who each year spend several weeks abroad helping in hospitals where the staffing situation is critical. In retirement we all need to do things that demand our best, even when no salary is paid. Too many wait for something to turn up, instead of going and turning up something!

Respect for the Elderly

Affection and care for the old, the helpless and the incurable
are the true gold mines of a culture.
Our high calling is to slip the key of a sympathetic imagination
into the closed door of someone's life, and enter into that
person's loneliness and perplexities.

Said the little boy, 'Sometimes I drop my spoon.'
Said the little old man, 'I do that too.'
The little boy whispered, 'I sometimes wet my pants.'
'I sometimes do that too,' laughed the little old man.
Said the little boy, 'I often cry.'
The old man nodded, 'So do I.'
'But worst of all,' said the boy, 'it seems grown ups don't pay attention to me.'
He felt the warmth of a wrinkled old hand.
'I know what you mean,' said the little old man.

❧

A shoe shop assistant was attending to an old lady. As he took off her shoes she apologised for her knobbly feet. 'Well, Madam', he said, 'you really cannot expect to have beauty at both ends.'

❧

I was initially surprised to learn that a young minister, who had been invited to conduct a short act of worship in a care home for the elderly, chose for her text the verses in Luke's Gospel about parents bringing their children to Jesus. She said, 'I cannot get over the fact that Jesus' disciples said on that occasion, "Get the children out of here."' 'In a way', said the minister, 'I can understand this. After all, children make a noise. They have to be cared for. They take up everybody else's time. Besides they cannot contribute much. They are so often just a burden... But Jesus said, *Let them alone, let them come. They are kingdom people.*' The old people nodded in agreement. The young minister never mentioned elderly people, but her hearers got the message.

❧

For centuries a strong tradition of respect for old age ran through the Judaeo-Christian culture. The rapid increase of the number of old folk in our communities may well be one reason for the reduction in the veneration of the elderly. Their scarcity value has fallen. Few things sadden me more than when I see elderly people being treated as though they no longer have a right to an opinion, when others insist on making major decisions for them, sure that they know what is best for them. For example, to insist on a bereaved parent moving from a community where they are well known and well integrated, to a house near to them, is often mistaken kindness. Whereas in their former community a visit to the shops, bowling green or church involved numerous conversations with neighbours and friends, in the new community they have no friendship network. The only people they know are their family. Family and carers ought to remember that the elderly person also has feelings, wishes and opinions, and most important, the right to be heard.

❧

I warm to an unknown author's poetic version of the Beatitudes for the elderly:

Blessed are they who understand,
  my faltering step and palsied hand.
Blessed are they who know my ears today,
  must strain to catch the things they say.
Blessed are they who seem to know,
  that my eyes are dim and my wits are slow.
Blessed are they with cheery smile,
  who stop to chat for a little while.
Blessed are they who never say,
  'You've told that story twice today.'
Blessed are they who know the ways,
  to bring back memories of yesterdays.
Blessed are they who make it known,
  that I'm loved, respected and not alone.

In many African countries the elderly are considered to be human libraries because of the wealth of experience they have gathered over the years. A Margaret Simey who when in her eighties visited her son in Lesotho was struck by how moved the people there were that her son should enjoy the exceptional good fortune of having such an old mother. A Mary Oto Lijadu who lives in Nigeria tells how villagers often visit the elders to get their help to resolve village matters, and to receive their blessing. This respect leads to a greater communal willingness to care for the elderly. In many African countries, the idea of putting older people into nursing homes is very foreign. It is considered a great blessing when an older family member lives with the family.

Mary goes on to tell how when her youngest son was thirteen years of age, he said to her, 'Mummy when you are old you can come and live with me, but remember if I am going out with my family I will have to leave you behind with the dog.' She responded with delight saying, 'Tayo, that is very thoughtful. I hope you will remember to leave some food for me as well as the dog!'

❧

An eighty-year-old lady, whose sons came to visit infrequently, felt all the classic signs of them wanting to leave shortly after they arrived. Though she knew they led very busy and involved lives, yet one day she said to a friend, 'It is strange how one mother can take care of six sons, and six sons seem reluctant to visit and take care of one mother.' What she really wanted to know was that she still mattered to them. It would have made her day had they whispered as they left, 'Mum, you are very precious to us.'

❧

People who are concerned to brighten the lives of the elderly, especially those confined to their home or a care-home, soon discover that love, gentleness, understanding and a willingness to listen, can work miracles. To restore an old house is exciting. To restore joy in a lonely heart is even more exciting.

❧

A madrigal in Shakespeare's *The Passionate Pilgrim* says, 'Age and youth cannot live together; Youth is full of pleasance, Age is full of care.' I would question that. Looking back on our years in Dornoch my wife and I are convinced that one of the best things we did with the youth group was teach them to play whist! Our aim was to bring them into closer contact with the elderly in the community. Once a month they challenged the residents of Oversteps, our local eventide home, to a whist drive. What happy occasions these were. The young people were desperate to beat the old folks, many of whom had been playing whist all their life. The old people were equally determined not to lose. Had we asked the young people simply to go and chat with the old folks, I strongly suspect it would have been a social disaster. But seated at card tables, and later at tea tables, there was a lot of friendly chatter and laughter. The generation gap was bridged.

After the young folk returned home, it was a joy to see and hear the residents, instead of sitting and simply gazing at each other, chatting excitedly about what had happened that night, about things the young people had said and done, and about the clothes they had been wearing. The evening had broadened their horizons. For their part the young people, by taking part, not only found satisfaction in having so obviously enriched the lives of the care home residents, but also a new respect for themselves. At least some of them learned that empathy, imagining what it is like to be in someone else's shoes, is a life-enriching quality

Shortly after becoming involved as chaplain in the life of Oversteps, I called one day to offer my congratulations to one of the residents, on her ninety-seventh birthday. I was amused to learn that earlier that day Mr Mackay, a former policeman, who at 104 was the oldest resident, had knocked on Mrs Philcox's door, shaken her warmly by the hand and said, 'Now remember you are just a young lassie!'

Senior Moments

'My secrets are safe with my old friends.
They cannot remember them.'

One of the very few advantages of a failing memory is that it helps some people deal with a troubled conscience.

For years I marvelled at the memory's powers of reproducing remote facts after so long an interval. Now I marvel at how inconsistent my memory has become. I have great sympathy for the young lad who defined memory as what you forget with. Senior moments are perhaps best described as mental blips that waylay us at the most inconvenient times. A very common problem is forgetting people's names, even people we know well. A minister friend, John Peterson in Pennsylvania, tells of a lady of 78 in his congregation who went to Florida for three months in the winter. She returned engaged to an elderly gentleman. When John heard this, he phoned to congratulate her. When he inquired about her fiancé's name there was a lengthy silence. 'You know I can't honestly remember. He is out at the moment, but I will phone you when he gets back.' A close friend tells how his mind went completely blank when asked by the lady in the Crieff Golf Shop the name of his new and first grand-daughter. His round of golf was ruined because he desperately kept trying to recall it. It was not until he was half-way home that he remembered it was Jessica.

Though my own memory is not in great shape, I am not as forgetful or confused as the Episcopal minister in the supermarket who one day saw a minister he knew well coming towards him. He could not for the life of him remember his name. Finally when they were very close he decided all he could do was shake hands. In doing this, he walked into a mirror!

A Mr Vaughan tells how he and his wife attended a business conference. During dinner he asked his wife three times the names of their table companions. When, on returning to the hotel, he asked her the same question, she chided him about his lack of attention. She ended her lecture by saying that she was surprised he could remember her name. With a mischievous twinkle in his eye, he responded, 'Why do you think I often call you darling?' Such stories remind me of the old man who during a discussion about the good old days said, 'I'd love to live in the past. My trouble is I cannot remember it.'

Three friends of approximately the same age, decided to celebrate their sixtieth birthdays with a meal in the Grand Hotel. They chose this hotel because it had young attractive waitresses who wore miniskirts. For their seventieth birthdays they returned to the Grand Hotel, because the wine and meals were of a high quality. For their seventy-fifth birthdays they again chose the Grand Hotel, because it had a disabled access. After much debate, they decided for their eightieth birthdays to have a meal in the Grand Hotel, because they had not been there before!

The American broadcaster Andy Rooney recalled how at the age of 83 he ate one night in a restaurant in Columbus. The following day he wished he could remember the name of the restaurant because with the experience of the night before, he wanted to remember not to eat there again!

Watching a television programme about marriage prompted a husband to ask his wife of 60 years, 'If you had it to do over again, would you marry me?' 'You have asked me that question before', she replied. When he then asked her what she had previously replied, she said, 'I don't remember.'

Though many retired people may not know the medical term 'Age Activated Attention Deficit Disorder', most of us know the reality. Two verses of doggerel express this disorder well.

My forgetter's getting better
But my rememberer is broke.
To you that may seem funny
But to me it is not a joke.
For when I am here, I'm wondering
If I really should be there.

Oft times I walk into a room and say
'Now what am I here for?'
I wrack my brain, but all in vain
A zero is my score.
Oft times I put something away
Where it is safe, but gee,
The person it is safest from is generally Me.

In another description of Age Activated Attention Deficit, a man describes what for him is now a typical day.

I decide to water the lawn. As I enter the garage to get the hose, I decide my dirty car needs washing. On reversing out the car, I notice there is mail in the porch. I get out, pick up the mail. I decide to open it before washing the car. I lay the car keys on the kitchen table, and put the junk mail in the rubbish bin under the sink. Noticing that the bin is now full, I decide to take out the garbage first. On returning I decide I had better pay the bills. Noticing there is only one cheque left, I head towards the study to get my other cheque book. On the way, a vase of flowers catches my eye. They need watering. As I fill a container with water I suddenly spot the remote control for the TV. Someone had left it on the kitchen table. I realise that tonight when we go to watch TV, I will be hunting for the remote, but by then I won't remember where it is, so I decide to put it back in the living room where it belongs, but first I will water the flowers. Some of it spills on the floor. So I set the remote back down on the table, get some towels and wipe up the water. Then I head down the hall trying to remember what I was planning to do.

At the end of the day; the lawn is not watered, the car isn't washed, the bills aren't paid, the flowers don't have enough water, I can't find the remote control, and I cannot remember what I did with the car keys.

The bad news is that if this is not you yet, the day is coming!

Though I am getting more forgetful
And mixed up in the head
I can assure you I'm still living
I am not yet among the dead.

I've got used to my arthritis
To my dentures I'm resigned
I can cope with my bi-focals
But – oh my – I miss my mind.

Sometimes I can't remember
When I'm standing by the stair
If I should be going up for something
Or have just come down from there.

And before the fridge, so often
My mind is full of doubt
Now did I put some food away
Or come to take some out?

❧

An irate elderly woman phoned her local newsagent, demanding to know why her Sunday paper had not been delivered. 'Madam,' the newsagent responded, 'Today is Saturday. Your Sunday paper will be delivered tomorrow – on Sunday!' After a lengthy pause, she said, 'So that is why no one was at church today.'

❧

A friend tells me he now writes down everything he wants to remember. That way instead of spending a lot of time trying to remember what he has to do or purchase, he spends the time wondering where he put the paper on which he wrote it down.

❦

After reading a book entitled *Aids to Better Memory*, a retired husband boasted that he was sure his memory was greatly improved. To test it, his wife asked him to repeat the list of things he was to put in the car for their trip the following day. With amazing accuracy he recited them. Next day as they were driving out of the garden, his wife asked, 'Can you still remember the list of things we were to bring?' Proudly he again repeated the list without a single omission. When she then asked him where they were, she received a gaping stare in reply!

❦

At a community supper for pensioners in Florida, one of the men present cast a few admiring glances at the woman opposite. Later that evening he asked her if she would consider marrying him. 'Yes, yes, I will,' she said excitedly. The meal ended with pleasant exchanges. Both went home. The following morning the old man was troubled. He could not remember whether she had said, I will or I won't. Fortunately he remembered her name. So he phoned her hoping she would be patient with him. 'I enjoyed our meal and time together last night, but I cannot remember whether when I asked you to marry me, you said Yes or No.' 'Oh,' she said, 'I remember I said Yes, and I meant it with all my heart. But I am so glad you called, because I could not remember who had asked me.'

While We Live, Let Us Live

He is so old that he does not watch programmes that end: 'to be continued'

He has not done anything except grow old – and look how long it took him to do that.

Abraham Lincoln is quoted as saying, 'In the end it's not the years in your life that count. It is the life in your years.' I warm to that and to the prayer of the old Scot, 'O Lord keep me alive while I am still living.'

❧

Many years ago a friend helped an old lady off a bus. As she set off down the street she turned and said to him in a stern tone of voice, 'Never grow old.' She obviously found the gradual deterioration of her bodily strength and physical faculties so frightening, humiliating and generally unpleasant that her advice was 'Never grow old.' Despite revolutionary (and often very costly) therapies, replacement organs and all the fat-sucking and wrinkle-removal treatments, the cells that make up our bodies still age, decay and die. Dr Lorna Layward of the medical trust Research into Ageing reminds us that 'There are no known interventions that will stop or reverse the ageing process in humans.'

❧

Ageing is the only way to live a long time. If we are always battling against becoming older, we are always going to be unhappy, because it will happen anyhow. Someone likened life to a camel. You can do anything with it, except make it back up. I remember hearing of a couple who were shopping in John Lewis. The wife was looking at a sleek but expensive home treadmill. Trying to convince her husband that they should buy it, she said, 'By using that, I could get back to looking the way I did when I first met you.' 'Jean', he said, 'it is an exercise machine, not a time machine.' We may age at different rates, but age we will.

❧

Abraham, one of the great Old Testament characters, is proof that there is life after seventy-five. In his seventies he continued to show that intrepid adventuresome spirit that many expect to find only in much younger people. Leaving his home in the north Arabian desert, he led a long migration across a hot, dry and desolate wilderness. His motto seems to have been that of the Romans centuries later, *Dum Vivimus Vivamus*, 'While we live, let us live.' History books are full of people whose greatest work was done in their later years – Alfred Hitchcock, Rembrandt, Bach and Jacques Cousteau to name but a few. Grandma Moses learned to paint in her old age. Thomas Edison, having invented not only the gramophone, the light-bulb, the microphone, mimeograph, storage batteries and having pioneered cinematography, at the age of 80 started studying botany, a science completely new to him.

❧

'Old men,' said T. S. Eliot 'ought to be explorers.' Far from being a place of the status quo, maturity ought to be a place of adventure where we try new things. The Danish philosopher Kierkegaard once said that to avoid becoming encrusted older people ought to imitate a good farmer. 'In life as well as in agriculture there is such a thing as rotation of crops.' I recall a conversation many years ago with a former Moderator of our National church, Dr Roy Sanderson. When I asked this amazingly youthful 94-year-old what he was doing these days, his answer thrilled me: 'I am taking a computer class.' This would help him, he said, to keep in contact with his children, grandchildren and great grandchildren. Dr McAfee Brown, one of my finest teachers, wrote his first novel at the age of 78 – *Dark the Night, Wild the Sea.*

❧

Ron Ferguson recalls the delight he experienced on reading how when the youthful Barack Obama became President, Senator Robert Byrd, aged ninety-one, announced that he would hand over the chairmanship of the Senate appropriations committee to Senator Daniel Inouye. Senator Inouye said he hoped he was sufficiently prepared to succeed his mentor. He was a mere eighty-four! So long as people retain reasonable health, old age can be a time of both achievement and enjoyment. A doctor tells how one of the major discoveries he made while in general practice was that 'busy people have less time to be ill.' A fatigued spirit makes an exhausted physique. When people say they are tired, they often mean, 'I am tired of the same routine.'

❧

When at the age of eighty Goethe wrote the second part of *Faust*, he was as youthful in heart as the bright young sorcerer of whom he wrote. In the early part of the drama, because Faust is bored, he makes a pact with the devil Mephistopheles. But instead of giving him a sense of lasting worth, Faust becomes more and more bored. Later as an older man, as chancellor of the empire, he undertakes to construct dykes to push the sea back, so that in place of stagnant swamps, green fields might appear. The men in his territory can then till the soil and grow food and rear cattle. When Faust observes the resultant joy of the people, he suddenly experiences an inner satisfaction he has never known before. 'I now enjoy', he said, 'the highest moment.' So too do those who continue to stretch their capabilities to the limit, who throw themselves into some worthwhile cause with complete dedication. Life continues to be for them a wonderful adventure.

❧

Get a life. Live, don't just exist. Do not lose the thrills of life because you are old. People become old because they have lost the thrill of life. It was said about John Wesley, 'So fine an old man I never saw. The happiness of his mind beamed in his countenance. While some people were charmed with his wisdom, others delighted in the brightness of his personality. In him old age was a delightful state.' There are few finer things old people can give to the world than radiant personalities.

The Face We Deserve

Like a white candle in a holy place
So is the beauty of an aged face

When Daniel Webster wished to give the impression of remembering someone from his past, he would often say, 'How is the old complaint?' From the often lengthy answer he was able to deduce who the person was! Whereas the negative complaints of cantankerous old people are numerous, their positive enthusiasms are often very few. Their conversation is full of reminiscences about all the disagreeable things that have happened to them. They nourish a chronic grievance against what they call 'their luck', or as the 17th-century writer Jeremy Taylor put it, 'they collect a bunch of thorns and sit down on them.' Writing about such grievance collectors, Bernard Levin said, 'If they had been present at the feeding of the five thousand, one would have complained that there was no lemon to go with the fish, and the other would have demanded more butter for the bread.' I warm to the question addressed by a waiter to an extremely disagreeable elderly patron, 'Is anything all right madam?' In a perceptive play of the 1960s Billy Fisher's grandmother is the classical crotchet of advanced years. All through the play her crabbiness bursts out again and again, leading to constant trouble between the generations.

Fortunately most of us have also known very gracious old folk who remind us of the proverb, 'The older the fiddle, the sweeter the tune.' Advancing years have mellowed them. It has made them less cocksure and less judgmental. The elderly Goethe said, 'I see no fault committed by others which I could not have committed myself.' I can recall faces, some of them lined with crow's-feet, which sparkled and shone like stained-glass windows when the sun was out. When the darkness set in, their beauty continued to be revealed by a light from within.

A young girl once remarked to her mother just after a white-haired lady with a lovely face left their home: 'If I could be as nice as she is – so lovely and so kind – I would not mind growing old.' 'Well,' said her mother, 'if you want to be like her you had better begin right now, for she did not become such a fine person in a hurry.'

Some would argue that beauty competitions should only be for people over 70. Whereas in your teens and twenties you have the face God gave you, 'after a certain age' as the French writer Camus said 'every person is responsible for their face.' Oscar Wilde's story, *The Picture of Dorian Gray* concerns a man whose life and deeds were evil, but whose face for a time preserved the appearance of honesty and kindness. But ultimately his features revealed the unlovely state of his heart. The quality of his inner life was finally etched on his countenance. So it was also with the debauched Lord Steyne in Thackeray's *Vanity Fair.* Thackeray describes his livid face with its 'ghastly eyes that gave no light, and seemed tired of looking out on a world of which almost all the pleasure and all the beauty had palled.' How very different it was with Gladys Aylward whose life was portrayed in the once popular television series, 'This is Your Life', and later in the film *The Inn of the Sixth Happiness.* As a young woman Gladys, who was scarcely five foot tall, was no beauty queen. She never had a boyfriend. Most of her life was spent toiling as a missionary in China, doing invaluable work with refugee children and hardened criminals. She suffered much, but what a trail of glory the love which all her life she had bestowed on others left on her face. I doubt if I have ever seen a more radiant and serene face on television. Her lovely interior attitudes had finally reached the surface. They had greatly enhanced her looks.

❦

There was more truth than we thought in our mother's remark, 'You had better watch in case the wind changes some day and your face remains like that.' Many a pretty face has been spoiled by continual discontent and whining. Hardening of the heart ages people as quickly as hardening of the arteries. Some spend their waking hours feeling sorry for themselves. A Dr Francis Brennan who has researched the links between happiness and immunity from disease says, 'Feeling down and sorry for ourselves increases our vulnerability to infection.' There really ought to be a daily limit put on self-pity. At most a few tearful moments, then on with the day. Most people don't want to hear our moans. A few might even be glad we have them!

Coping with Change

One of the great things about children is that they do not constantly speak of yesterday. Their interests are of today and tomorrow.

To something new we are inevitably hostile until it has had the edge taken off by it being imitated at least twice.

When at the age of a hundred the Queen Mother presented prizes at a senior citizen's gardening competition, she said, 'Is it me, or are the elderly getting younger these days?' Calling people 'elderly' never used to cause a stir, but today some take issue with the term. Though one can understand the upset of those who are called elderly at age 60, I have more difficulty understanding those over 75 who are critical of the term. When Clement Freud was asked if he objected to being called elderly, he said that at his age, he was glad to be called 'alive'. When Freud stood for the post of Rector at St Andrews University, some of the supporters of the other candidates, at a hustings meeting, questioned whether he was not in fact too old to represent students. Clement replied, 'A great deal has been made of the fact that I'm seventy-eight. Don't worry as this is an entirely temporary situation. Next year I fully intend to be seventy-nine.' He certainly did not equate being elderly with taking up permanent residence in an armchair or bed, and dribbling.

It is a strange feeling for those who have led busy and active lives to find themselves freed from the routine of the working day, or suddenly in a backwater. Retirement involves breaking the crust of habit, which is never easy. It involves having to settle for less contact with valued colleagues, with marked changes in former daily routines, and a reduction in income. This can result in a cut in luxuries, fewer meals out, less expensive holidays, and sometimes moving to a smaller house. No more the dream of one day owning a Jaguar and a country cottage.

The person who says he is too old to change probably always was. Some, like Walter de la Mare's old Jim Jay, 'get stuck fast in yesterday.' The habits and attitudes of yesterday having become frozen, they find it almost impossible to cope with the physical, psychological, social, emotional and financial changes, which are part and parcel of retirement. Some retired husbands become their wives' full time jobs!

Others, who cope reasonably well with such necessary adjustments, are unwilling to change any of the prejudices with which they grew up. As the body sometimes reacts strongly to strange foods, so they distrust new ideas. If people were honest they would admit that they often begin to argue against new ideas, even before they have been completely stated. Mentally wanting a cosy retirement, they keep reading newspapers that reinforce their very definite views. They are sure that to change their mind would be a sure sign of instability and insecurity. I sometimes suspect that when people say to me 'that was a good sermon' what they mean is that it was a sermon that confirmed everything they already believed or felt.

Having said that, I must admit I find it heartening to meet reasonably healthy old folk who sometimes resist the unnecessary changes that their families seek to impose on them. They resist, not because they are old, but because they are young enough in spirit still to covet independence and freedom of choice. Instead of being the sweet, little old ladies that society sometimes tries to make them, they continue to be the same spunky rebels they have always been. Mark you, in their resistance to change and to offers of help, there is no need to be as dour, intolerant, stubborn and unreasonable as Victor Meldrew in 'One Foot in the Grave'. 'I gave a young boy down the road a swift cuff on the ear for trying to help me across the road. It will be only a matter of time before they are forcing me on a day trip to Eastbourne.'

Walking the World with Gratitude

Solzhenitsyn who experienced the awful horrors of the Gulag wrote years later, 'If your back is not broken, if your feet can walk, if both arms can bend, if both eyes can see and both ears hear, then whom should we envy. And why? Our envy of others devours us most of all. Rub your eyes and purify your heart and prize above all else in the world those who love you and who wish you well.'

The road of life is littered with astonishments. A naturalist once said that every time he took people into the woods, he emerged with a deepened conviction that there was only one classification of people which was really significant – the classification of the quick and the dead. The quick were those with sensitive antennae which reach out to enjoy the astonishing beauty and pageant of the natural world. The dead are those who stumble through life blindfolded, who seldom use their senses. The next time you feel jaded, I suggest that instead of wallowing in your misery, you take 'a short walk of thanks'. What enchantment there is in the commonplace for all who care to look for it. The world is full of wonders to non-glazed eyes. Keep them open. There is much to see. 'Consider the lilies,' said Jesus, 'Behold the birds of the air.' Smell the dew and the rain. Enjoy the rainbow with its seven sisters of coloured lights. Sit down and listen to the surf at the beach. On a clear autumn night, watch the trail of the stars, the path of the full moon, rising like an orange balloon and turning to silver as it rises. In the spring, watch the gradual changes on the branches of trees. Get up occasionally at dawn and enjoy first light.

I become more and more convinced that happiness is less the result of the occasional great gift of fortune, than the thousand little joys of every day – family ties, books, health, sleep, songs, a word of thanks or encouragement, warmth in the winter, memories in old age. Robert Louis Stevenson said, 'To miss the joy is to miss all.' This being so, try saying to yourself, 'Suppose I will never experience again a warm piece of buttered toast, or salt-laden air at the beach, or a glorious sunset, or a full moon hanging in a black sky on a frosty night, or the glimpse of a red-tailed hawk circling above, or the great variety of bird song.' As you grow older, don't let your reaction to such commonplace things grow dull. Don't take for granted the wonder of a baby's smile or the delight of watching a two-year-old concentrate as she tries to pick up a Cheerio with her thumb and first finger, or the joy of having a meal and a laugh with people we love and value. Some have found it helpful before going to bed to jot down the things which that day made them grateful or brought a smile to their face. The habit of feeling grateful gives people a better quality of life. At the age of ninety-three Pablo Casals wrote, 'Age is a relative matter. If you continue to work and to absorb the beauty in the world about you, you find that age does not necessarily mean getting old.' Eric Hoffer, in his book *Reflections on the Human Condition*, points out that 'the hardest arithmetic to master is that which enables us to count our blessings.'

How precious are close friendships, people who genuinely care about us, about what we think, what we feel and what we suffer. Everybody has to be somebody to somebody to be anybody. Friends to whom you can pour out the content of your heart, chaff and grain together, are an indispensable ingredient of a full and happy life. Whereas acquaintances want to share your prosperity, true friends insist on sharing your adversity.

❦

What a precious gift health also is. It is often not until we begin to lose our health, that we really value it. 'Good health is a crown that too often only the sick and the elderly can see.' How fortunate I have been to live long enough to have laughter lines etched into deep grooves on my face, and to have grandchildren, for many die before a grandchild is born. Diphtheria, tuberculosis and measles were common life-threatening illnesses when I was a boy. Trivial infections would often prove fatal. A walk in an old graveyard is a powerful reminder that our ancestors often had more dead children than we have live ones. Let us never forget that health is wealth, and it is tax-free.

I am also glad that I have lived long enough to enjoy a warm double-glazed home, brighter lights and much swifter travel. I am glad sewage is no longer considered treated, if dumped in a river. I rejoice that more and more waste is being recycled. I am glad that despite pollution, noise and over-crowding, the world is still adorned with great beauty.

I find it difficult to count all my blessings, one of which is surely that I no longer have to do all the counting – computers and calculators do it for me. Computers also make it easier to make corrections to manuscripts. No longer do I have to tear sheets of paper out of the typewriter and throw them away as I used to do.

When I was a boy we made telephones by stretching waxed string between two empty cylindrical tins. We made a small hole in the bottom of each tin, put the string through, knotted it at each end, and then talked to each other at a distance of about fifty feet. I am glad I have lived long enough to communicate far more efficiently by e-mail, fax and mobile phone. Skype has allowed me to see and talk to my son and his family in Seattle, six thousand miles away. Television has made me far more aware of what is happening in distant corners of the world.

With the passing years I have become more and more aware of my indebtedness, to great composers and artists, to novelists and film makers, to saints and heroes, to inventors and medical pioneers. The civic motto of Belfast is 'Pro tanto quid retribuamus'. In spite of the local translation 'How much can you get for a quid?' it really means, 'In return for so much what shall we give?' Behind the motto is the thought that the person who is aware of his indebtedness will be more likely to feel constrained to be a better citizen. 'We ought because we owe'. I smiled recently when I saw on the back window of a van, a new version of the song of the seven dwarfs – 'I owe, I owe, so off to work I go.' In so many spheres of life our acknowledgement of debt strengthens our sense of obligation and determination to work harder. In his biography of St Francis of Assisi, G. K. Chesterton wrote, 'It is the highest and holiest of paradoxes that the person who really knows he cannot pay his debt will be forever paying it.'

What I Have Learned

When the body is tired, we should exercise the mind, and when the mind is tired, we should exercise the body.

As I have grown older I have learned,

that life is a mixture of good days and bad days, give and take, success and failure.

that there are things we should allow to go over our heads like water off a duck's back.

that one should keep envy in check, for it destroys so much that is fine in people.

that it is vitally important to praise and encourage others

that you cannot hug your children or wife too often.

that we sometimes have to reject a passing pleasure for a higher good.

that though many of the things we do appear insignificant, it is important we do them well.

that honesty is more important than profitable subterfuge.

that buck-passing usually turns out to be a boomerang.

that those who lose their temper usually lose out.

that the young can be just as heavy-laden, anxious and depressed as the old.

that you must not let bad times make you bitter.

that the best tranquiliser is a clear conscience.

that every person now and then has burnt toast for breakfast.

that carrying a chip on your shoulder is the easiest way to get into a quarrel or fight.

that when you forgive, you release a prisoner, and that prisoner is you.

that it really does not matter who gets the credit as long as the enterprise benefits.
that it is only through cooperative effort that we move on to better things.
that there are two types of people, those who go into a room effectively announcing 'Here I am' and those who go in and say 'Ah there you are.'
that there are those who, as Oscar Wilde said, have the gift of perpetual old age, who are never young.
that there is truth in the phrase 'the advantages of disadvantages'.
that luxuries are what other people buy.
that there is no harm in smiling and saying 'Good Morning', even when it is freezing or pouring with rain.
that to have good friends is to have the greatest of all gifts.
that true love is love that has no exchange of payment.
that folks are no harder to get along with in one place than another, or one church than another.
that 'getting along' with other people depends to a large extent on our behaviour and attitude.
that even when we are 'over the hill', that does not mean we cannot enjoy the view.
that those who are great at remembering a joke, can't remember how many times they have already told it to you.
that the newspapers you spread on the floor to keep it clean are often such fascinating reading.

Can We Live Longer?

'Live rather than avoid death. Life is not breath but action.'
Jean Jacques Rousseau

'Laughter is the sun that drives winter from the human face.'
Victor Hugo

Ageing is often a matter of the mind.
If you don't mind it does not matter!

Some believe that many of the detrimental health changes that occur in people as they get older, are in large part caused by progressive protein and other nutritional deficiencies. In her book *Stop Aging Now – the ultimate plan for staying young*, Jean Carper devotes several chapters to the role of supplements such as Vitamins C and E and Beta Carotene, which she describes as an all-round anti-aging anti-oxidant. Other chapters in the book are devoted to the role of calcium, chromium, zinc and magnesium. She also writes at length about the Asian secret of long life – soya beans – and tea, the ancient longevity drink. I would not for a minute deny that there are health benefits in some of these supplements, but I become more and more convinced that there are also powerful psychological and genetic factors why some people age rapidly and others retain their vigour.

Inheriting a strong constitution is one factor. Another is regular exercise. Our cardiovascular system, physical vigour and mental alertness benefit by exercising regularly. Strong family ties, not too much emotional stress and the determination to make full use of our mind and faculties when we retire, can also help extend people's life-span. Social interests such as choral singing are also therapeutic. Strathclyde University now run a course entitled 'Health and Well-Being in Song.' The lecturer on choral singing speaks not only of the power of choral music to reduce fatigue, but its wonderful tingle factor!

For years I have written and spoken extensively about the beneficial effects of laughter, kindly humour, and a love of fun. All three help stimulate parts of the brain. They play a major role in helping people maintain physical and psychological health. They are a kind of social salt adding savour to life. Joanne Woodward said, 'Sexiness wears thin after a while, and beauty fades, but to be married to a man who makes you laugh regularly is a real treat.' Laughter has been justifiably likened to internal aerobics. It is generally recognised that patients who laugh often and heartily, especially at themselves, have a better chance of recovery from illness than those who take themselves far too seriously. Laughter and positive thinking can produce pharmaceutical marvels. According to Professor William Fry of Stanford University, 'laughter, playfulness and relaxation increase blood flow.' He also says that 'a hundred hearty laughs is the aerobic equivalent of ten minutes on a rowing machine'. Watching re-runs of 'Faulty Towers' and 'Morecambe and Wise' may in fact be almost as good for us as going jogging. Never be afraid to laugh at yourself. After all as Dame Edna Everage once said, 'We could be missing out on the joke of the century!'

The mind is the supreme organ of the body. Our mental state controls the activities and energies of the rest of the body. How we feel about ourselves is the linchpin of quality life in our later years. A buoyant outlook on life is crucial. People who regularly exercise their chuckle muscles, who have a cheerful disposition, and sing as they journey through life, are on average likely to live as long, if not longer, than those who put their trust in supplements. Humour and fun help unlock creative powers for living. So too does faith, insight into life's meaning, insight that generates power, insight that brings one into humble but happy service to God and others.

17th-Century Food for Thought

Dean Swift, the author of *Gulliver's Travels*, has an interesting article entitled:

'Resolutions when I come to be old.'

Not to neglect decency or cleanliness.
Not to hearken to flatteries, nor conceive that I can be beloved by a young woman.
Not to be over severe with young people, but make allowances for their youthful follies and weaknesses.
Not to tell the same story over and over again to the same people.

In a prayer found in Rochester Cathedral, a 17th-century nun suggested other resolutions for those growing old.

Not to think I must say something on every subject and every occasion.
Not to be cock-sure when my memory seems to clash with the memories of others.
Not to use our vast store of wisdom to straighten out everybody's affairs!
Not to rehearse our aches and pains.
Not to be moody or bossy.

An ancient document from the same era records this conversation, 'Cousin', said she, 'do you believe I am in the right when I say that I am but fifty.' 'I ought not to dispute it, Madam,' replied he, 'for I have heard you say so these past ten years.'

Age — Not a Good Beautician

My body is adjusting
To years of attack
My waistline's pushing forward
While my hair-line's falling back

'I have still got the figure I had at twenty. The trouble is that everything is now four inches lower.'

'I don't mind telling people I am 75. I just mind being it.'

Vanity and narcissism are major problems with some elderly folk – the compulsive need to be admired and praised. They yearn for continued recognition of what they once were – the athlete, scholar or beauty queen. Some build shelves for silver trophies and medals, and make wall space for framed citations. Former beauties have the greatest difficulty, for though time may be a great healer, it is not a good beautician. 'In Hollywood,' said Barry Norman, 'the second worst sin is to be old; the very worst is to look old.' A portrait painter observed that most women are satisfied with their portrait if it makes them look ten years younger. Some women become obsessed with their fading attractiveness, with rediscovering the fountain of youth. They want others to keep noticing them and saying, 'She is so beautiful... She looks so young.' There are however few more embarrassing sights than that of people who, as the age for a free bus pass approaches, indulge in obsessive self-maintenance, who in a desperate attempt to recover former charms, plaster their faces with costly cosmetics and purchase clothes designed for far younger people. You can say few more damaging things about a woman than that she looks like mutton dressed up as lamb. I remember hearing of two farmers who were one day walking down Union Street in Aberdeen. Approaching them was a fashionable woman in her early thirties, very heavily made up. When one of the farmers commented on what an attractive woman she was, the other said, 'No, with all that top dressing, the ground beneath cannot be very good.'

How often it is the good-looking folk, the ones who need the least help with their appearance, who go in for obsessive body-maintenance. Britain now has a multi-million pound cosmetic surgery industry. Every day hundreds go under the knife for face-lifts, or pay handsomely for Botox injections into the muscles that create wrinkles around the eyes, forehead and neck. Joan Rivers once said that she wished she had had an identical twin, so that she could have known what she would have looked like without plastic surgery. Though such surgery may result in people looking different and sometimes even younger, they do not always look the better for it. In a recent article the TV presenter Gaby Roslin tells how, if you look your age, it is harder to get work in the TV and film industries. At one stage she did contemplate Botox treatment, but finally decided against it. She asked herself, 'Why am I so ashamed to look my age?' She continued, 'I am not telling anyone not to have the injections. All I am saying is why not embrace the fact that we are healthy, and yes we are getting older. There are lots of creams around. Go outside and get some exercise. Walk whenever you can. Drink water.' I agree. If women look their age, they more often than not look better than if they try to do more about it than regularly having their hair done, dressing attractively and wearing a few pieces of appropriate jewellery. Simple necklaces can distract minds from wrinkles! An alternative way of looking at our reflection in the mirror is to look for the interesting signs and designs that maturing experiences have drawn on our faces, and hopefully glimpse there the legacy of inner attitudes which have motivated us, and the measure of self we have given to others and to good causes.

Another obsession with some elderly folk is hoarding money even when they have no heirs and little prospect of using anything like all of it. A 93-year-old lady, who lived in sheltered accommodation, became very anxious about the state of her finances, even though she had ample savings. When her son-in-law tried to ease her mind by telling her that, given her likely expenses, she had more than enough money to last the next sixteen years, she replied, 'That's fine but how will I manage after that?' Many like that lady base their financial calculations on the possibility of living until they are 110. A brother and sister I used to visit were the last two survivors of a family of six. None of the family had married and each had left their estate to the others. The last time I visited them it was a bitterly cold winter's day. The only source of heat in their living room was a one-bar radiator. When they both died, I learned that their estate was worth several millions! I wonder if they found comfort in watching their bank balances increase while their other powers were dwindling.

Sunshine and Shadow

Discovered among the papers in Thomas Edison's desk was the quotation, 'When down in the mouth, remember Jonah – he came out all right.'

There are times in the journey of life when the sun shines brightly on our path, when we are so lyrically happy we virtually fly. But there are other times when sunshine is followed by shadow. Major bumps bring us down to earth. Though for fifty years I have had close dealings with people in times of crises, I am no nearer understanding the why of suffering. But what I have learned is that setback and adversity either make a person smaller or bigger.

The depletion of vital energies, the termination of accustomed tasks, the death of family members and close friends, increasing ills of the body and other factors make despondency a common problem with elderly folk. Anyone who expects completely to escape such setbacks is asking the impossible. To be sad in bereavement, disheartened by disappointment, dismayed by the world's greed and cruelty, disconsolate when personal trust is betrayed, that is natural. We all have cellars in our emotional houses, but don't let us take up permanent residence there.

I never cease to marvel at what has been achieved by a positive rather than a negative attitude in difficult or painful circumstances, by a sufferer's determination to make the best of what is often second best, to go on living with dignity, courage, humour and composure. A man who studied the Inuit tribe wrote, 'Here was a people living in the most rigorous climate in the world, in the most depressing surroundings imaginable, haunted by famine in a grey sombre landscape... shivering in their tents in autumn, fighting recurrent blizzards in winter, toiling fifteen hours a day merely to get food and stay alive. Whereas one might have expected them to be melancholy, they were a cheerful people, always laughing.' Many of us have known friends, neighbours and fellow-workers who in desperate situations – afflicted by an incurable disease, or the victim of a financial disaster or some domestic tragedy, have continued to display an undefeated spirit. Few things are more impressive than to see quiet uncomplaining cheerfulness radiate from a sufferer's eyes and sometimes shrunken frame, to watch such people continue to think of life as a series of challenges.

❧

One night as Sir Harry Lauder, the famous Scottish entertainer, left the theatre, he was handed a telegram informing him that his son had been killed in the war. When interviewed about his great loss, he said, 'When a man has a great sorrow, he can turn sour on life, or turn to drink, or turn to God.' Harry chose the third option. Three weeks later he was on his way to France to entertain the troops, with such songs as, 'Keep right on to the end of the road.'

❧

At seventy-eight, Goya was deaf and his eyesight was failing. In order to work he had to wear several pairs of spectacles. But he continued to produce splendid work in a new style. When Sir Walter Raleigh was imprisoned in the Tower of London, he decided to use his time to write a 'history of the world'. He brightened the last days of his life by letting his mind roam up and down the centuries. John Bunyan, a prisoner in Bedford jail for conscience' sake, similarly escaped from the claustrophobic atmosphere of his prison cell, his own infirmities, and the awful pain of being separated from his wife and children, by writing the *Pilgrim's Progress*, by immersing himself in the great drama of God and human life.

❧

Dean Sperry of Harvard once wrote to a friend, who in the dark hours of a lingering illness, had been deserted by someone dear to him, 'John don't let your trouble get away from you, until you have somehow wrested a blessing out of it.' One of the lessons I quickly learned in the ministry was that faith is no insurance against setback or suffering. The pain of the faithful is not removed just because they are faithful. But having said that, how often a deep faith has helped them not only handle setbacks creatively, but become a channel of grace in the world. In time of trouble many have found that the greatest help and understanding come from those who have themselves been through the fires of personal suffering and have emerged from the experience a little wiser and more compassionate.

❧

Why God did not arrange it that we could have strength without strain, courage without conflict, greater understanding and tenderness without suffering, I don't know. But that is how it seems to be. Ernest Hemingway, despite his almost pathological devotion to the cult of violence, had the grace to say in his book *A Farewell to Arms*, 'The world breaks everyone and afterwards many are strong at the broken places.' That was certainly true of the psychiatrist Victor Frankl. His account of life as a prisoner in Auschwitz is both chilling and inspiring. Though many of his family members lost their lives in the camp's gas chambers, he never gave up his belief that the horror he had experienced could one day be transformed into something of value. He often quoted a remark of Nietzsche, 'That which does not kill me can make me stronger.' Wringing our hands ought not to stop us from rolling up our sleeves. Just as the wounded oyster mends itself with pearl, so courage in our own trouble and kindness in another's, can produce depth of character.

❧

David Paterson was one of the Scottish soldiers who towards the end of the Second World War helped liberate Holland. Fifty years later the survivors were invited to return and be thanked by Queen Beatrix. Jack Webster tells how as the pipes and the drums of the King's Own Scottish Borderers, followed by former members of the Royal Scots, the Glasgow Highlanders and the Commandos, headed toward the beach where they had landed, there was spontaneous applause. As the now elderly Davie, who had lost an arm in the liberation, was wheeled through the town, he smiled and waved to the crowds, 'I have come to look for my arm.' Impressed by his courage, humour and lack of bitterness, the Dutch women rushed and embraced him.

Senior Golfers

The Golfer's Prayer: 'May I live long enough to shoot my age.'

One of the golf's most attractive aspects is that it affords healthy exercise for all, sufficient for the young and yet not too strenuous for the retired. It offers challenge and excitement. It strengthens flabby muscles. Golfers who reach the allotted span are generally fitter than non-golfers of the same age. Golf cannot be learned too soon, and it is never too late to begin. The day after Tom Watson came so close to winning the Open at the age of fifty-nine, a fact marvelled at by the world's media, Terry Wogan, in his popular morning radio programme, pointed out that some people take up golf for the first time in their late fifties! One such was the distinguished broadcaster Alistair Cooke. Quickly succumbing to the lure of the game, golf became his greatest sporting passion. He played until well into his nineties. By that time his drives we are told were so short that he could 'hear the ball land'!

Not all geriatric golfers get, however, as much enjoyment out of the game as Alistair Cooke did. In one of his books he tells of a dogged old member of Cypress Point, who at the first hole one Saturday pulled his drive, topped his five wood, fluffed his chip into a bunker and finally took four putts on the green. He straightened up and looked at Alistair in utter amazement. 'What am I doing here? I don't have to do this. I am a rich man.' How mistaken non-golfers often are in assuming that every time their spouses are on the golf course they are having enormous fun. What mental anguish they often suffer. The elderly Bob Hope once said,

'I get upset over a bad shot like everyone else. But I now realise it is silly to let the game get to you. Now when I miss a shot, I just think what a beautiful day it is and what pure fresh air I am breathing. Then I take a deep breath. That is what gives me the strength to break the club.'

One elderly gentleman on being asked, at the end of his round, how he had got on, replied that he been off his game. But then he quickly added, 'Come to think of it, I am never on my game.' What refreshing honesty.

A John Finch tells how his father's golf game was less than inspiring. It was not surprising therefore that on a club outing he was assigned one of younger inexperienced caddies. At the first, a short par 4, he took 8. At the second his drive landed deep in the rough. His shot to the green being blocked by a huge tree, he turned to the caddie and said, 'What club do you think I should use?' 'I don't know sir,' came the reply. 'I don't play golf either.'

When Lee Trevino informed his wife that he was thinking of retiring from the professional circuit, she is reported to have said, 'Look Lee, these clubs don't have any idea how old you are.'

On the Sunday before the Open Championship which was held at Muirfield in 1935, a special Golfer's service was held in St Peter's Church in Gullane. Many of the past Open Champions, now all elderly, were present – Braid, Vardon, Herd and Massey. J. H. Taylor who, as well as being a five times Open Champion, was a much respected warden in the Anglican Church, read one of the lessons. The sermon title on that auspicious occasion was 'The Links of Life'. The preacher's four imaginative headings were: The course we play on; The clubs we carry; The hazards we encounter; The card we return.

❧

Since 1992 Denis Rice, a retired ethics lecturer, has collected from the rough at Montrose golf links, over 70,000 lost golf balls. Obviously not all Montrose golfers are of the calibre of Colin Montgomery or Paul Lawrie! 76-year-old Denis has become a walking advertisement for keeping fit in retirement as well as giving a helping hand to the Montrose professional and the local Oxfam group, who both receive the fruits of his labours. As a golf-ball finding machine he is well aware of the perils of his calling. Clad in several pairs of old trousers and thick gloves, he ploughs through prickly gorse bushes, brambles and nettles in his search. Some Montrose senior golfers, well aware that they will probably lose at least one ball during their round, have taken to writing 'Hello Denis' on their ball before driving from the first tee.

❧

When at the age of seventy-eight Arnold Palmer hit the first ball in the Masters out into a dense Augusta fog, he turned to the crowd and said he was glad he could still hit the ball out of sight! Stuart Dickson, a lifelong friend of Arnold's and his first wife Winnie, told me how, two years after Winnie died of cancer, Arnold became friendly with a lovely lady, Kit Gawthrop. One night when the four of them had arranged to have dinner together, Stuart and Arnold were standing at the lounge window. Kitty and Joanne were in the kitchen. Arnold who was obviously head over heels in love with Kitty, said to Stuart, 'I would do anything for her, I would take her anywhere she wanted to go, I would give her anything she wanted...' Overhearing this, Kitty put her head round the door and said, 'Arnold, all I want is your name!'

❧

Henry Longhurst was not only one of the finest golf writers and commentators of the 20th century, he was also for many years a scratch golfer. When as he got older, having developed the yips, he decided to give up the game and concentrate on his writing and broadcasting. Some time later he was diagnosed as having bowel cancer, and informed that he would have to have a colostomy – an artificial orifice inserted into his side. On hearing this he decided, in Hamlet's words, to 'shuffle off this mortal coil.' He acquired sufficient pills and a bottle of Glenmorangie highland malt whisky. The latter was to make swallowing the pills easier, and help him slide away peacefully. But so delightful and powerful was the Highland nectar, that he miscalculated the number of pills required. After admission to the Royal Sussex County Hospital the devoted staff there performed the necessary operation. They also later restored him physically to the 'normal channels'. When he later narrated this story in his *Sunday Times* golf column, inferring that Glenmorangie whisky had saved his life, the Tain distillery sent him every Christmas a large bottle of their product. The directors were in no doubt that it was one of the best free adverts they had ever had.

❦

It was in his fifties that Andrew Carnegie, the American steel magnate caught the golf bug. Fortunately the St Andrew's Golf Club in Hastings-on-Hudson was only an hour from his luxurious Manhattan home. Carnegie was elected to membership of the Club in 1896. In the early 1900s, after personally endorsing the club's new mortgage, Carnegie built himself a weekend cottage on the club property. In their little 'Golf cottage', he and his wife Louise spent many quiet and happy days. When he later bought and rebuilt Skibo Castle, four miles from Dornoch in the North of Scotland, he arranged for a nine-hole course to be built in the castle grounds. The club-house had to have a heather roof. He then invited J.H. Taylor, the five times Open Champion, who regularly holidayed in Dornoch, to come to the Castle and give his wife and himself golf lessons. There is unfortunately no record of the size of cheque Taylor received.

Despite golf lessons from an Open Champion, golf continued to be for Carnegie a series of tragedies obscured by occasional miracles. Fairways seemed to repel his ball, hazards continued to attract it. In a tribute to Carnegie entitled *He was a Weaver's Lad*, John Finley, who like Carnegie was also a happy hacker, recalls his first and last game with Carnegie at Skibo. It was at the beginning of the

First World War, a war which broke Carnegie's heart. He had worked so hard and invested so much money in the cause of peace. 'We had played a few holes when my conscience, beginning to trouble me, provoked me to question whether I ought to be out in the country away from my work, playing golf.' 'Oh,' Carnegie said, quick as a flash, 'Pritchett and I will both certify that you were not really playing golf!' Shortly after their game finished, a game which Carnegie probably suspected would be his last in Scotland, he presented Finley with his putter to which he had attached a note in his own handwriting, 'A very close game: couldn't have been closer so equally and badly we play.'

The fact that Carnegie was never a good golfer did not detract from his love of the game. At age seventy-five he wrote, 'It is played under the sky... Every breath seems to drive away weakness and disease... There is no Doctor like Doctor Golf.' The social aspect of the game also appealed to him. 'The oftener men meet on the golf course,' he said, 'the fonder they become of each other.'

Go on

Some years ago I was interviewed by Sir Harry Secombe in Skibo Castle. By that time he was in his early seventies. The subject of the interview was humour and faith. While the cameras and microphones were being set up we spent a delightful forty minutes seated on a couch sharing experiences, stories and anecdotes. He told me how when he was knighted by the Queen, he was told to return his passport to get it altered from Mr to Sir Harry Secombe. He naively thought he would be given a new passport, but instead the old one was returned with Mr struck out, and 'Now Sir' written in. A few months later when he visited Thailand the female immigration officer, having checked his passport and papers, said to him, 'I hope you have a good holiday Now Sir.'

During our time together I commented on his lovely signet ring. When he explained that the engraving was his own personal coat of arms, I inquired as to his motto. 'Go on', he said. Then he added, 'You can read it as "Goon" if you like.' I warm to that motto 'Go on' – Don't Quit. Many undertakings demand great patience. Madame Curie's success in finally isolating radium came out of her perseverance in the face of many failures. It was no different with one of Scotland's greatest scientists, Lord Kelvin. 'One word,' he said, 'characterises my strenuous efforts for the advancement of science during fifty-five years. That word is failure.' Though many of his early experiments did not succeed, he did not quit. He kept going.

A Highland minister told how one day a group of people in his parish were talking about heroism. They were saying that everybody sooner or later had to practise some kind of heroism. A young man in the group turned to a very ordinary, yet amazingly serene elderly woman who was present. What he did not know was that life for her had been a series of tragic happenings. 'And what kind of heroism do you practise?' the young man asked. The tone of the question clearly indicated that he did not believe that there could be any kind of heroism in a life like hers. She replied, 'I practise the heroism of going on.' All credit to those in every sphere of life, who when they experience days when the whole enterprise in which they are involved seems in doubt and the outcome trembles in the balance, bravely 'go on'.

When the brave Protestant pastor Martin Neimöller was arrested and sent to Dachau for speaking out against the Nazi treatment of the Jews, his old father emerged from retirement as a minister to proclaim the same truths as those for which his son had been arrested. He was determined the protests would go on.

❧

Lord Shaftesbury, having fought for years to reform the factory laws and promote the Mines Act, might have been excused if in his later years he had rested from his labours. In his seventies he fought to help the poor dress-makers and flower women of Piccadilly. At the age of 83 he became President of the Ragged School Union, a union which provided education for 300,000 poor children who roamed the streets of London.

In an amazing tribute to Booker T. Washington, Andrew Carnegie described him as 'perhaps the most remarkable man living today, taking into account his birth as a slave. He is the combined Moses and Joshua of his people. Not only has he led his people to the promised land, but still lives to teach them by example and precept how properly to enjoy it. He is one of those extraordinary men who rise at rare intervals and work miracles... History will tell of two Washingtons, the white and the black. One the father of his country, the other the leader of his race.' I recall Andrew Carnegie's daughter Margaret proudly showing me what the elderly Booker T. Washington had written in her autograph book when she was ten years of age, 'My dear young friend, I have learned that success is to be measured not so much by the position that one has reached in life, as by the obstacles one has overcome while trying to succeed.'

The Age of Discretion

A bell is no bell until you ring it,
A song is no song until you sing it,
And love in your heart was not put there to stay,
Love is not love until you give it away.

Faith, hope and love, but the greatest of these is love – St Paul

When the Hollywood legend Kirk Douglas was at the peak of his acting career, he stopped one night to offer a lift to a young soldier heading back to his army base. After settling in to the car the soldier turned and looked at his driver. There followed a double-take, before the young lad asked, 'Do you know who you are?' Though Kirk Douglas smiled, the question was one to which all his life he had sought an answer. 'When I became a movie actor I suddenly had to deal with fame and money and playing so many roles. I lost myself. I said, "Who am I?"' At the age of ninety Kirk Douglas felt it was time for yet another 'audit of his life'. Two years later he went public with the results of that audit, putting on a one-man show in Los Angeles: 'Before I Forget.' From the stage he spoke not just about his acting career, but about his near brushes with death as a result of a helicopter crash, his suicidal thoughts after a stroke, and the death of his youngest son Eric from an accidental drug overdose.

He recalled with fondness some words of his mother which for many years he had put on the back burner. 'A beggar must give something to another beggar who is worse off than he.' In an interview in *Newsweek*, he spoke of how the ageing process had brought him a deeper wisdom, a less combative stance and a new value system. 'Now in my golden years I have learned that you cannot know how to live until you know how to give.' What personal satisfaction he has of late derived from providing safe playgrounds for the children of Los Angeles, a recovery centre for women addicted to alcohol, and a Kirk Douglas theatre to develop the talents of young actors.

But for him the greatest bonus of old age, he said, has been 'the discovery of the true meaning of love. When I was younger my sense of love was not very deep. I was too involved with my career. Growing older brought me closer to my wife. It was like looking at her for the first time. I got to know who she really was and she really got to know me. Now I am much more romantic than I was years ago when so much of my life was spent portraying other characters on the screen.'

❧

Dr Archie Craig had a very distinguished career in the church. He served not only as chaplain to Glasgow University, but as Moderator of the General Assembly of the Church of Scotland. I have known few people who grew old as gracefully as Archie Craig. In their eighties, he and his wife Mary began to suffer from what he described as 'multiple disseminated annodominitis'. Their memories for names, and for things read, lost their fly-paper stickability. Unfortunately his wife's memory leaked much faster than his. She would repeat the same question within a few minutes. She finally was unable physically to manage even simple household tasks. Archie's patience with her was quite remarkable. When one evening in a very confused state she asked him, 'Does the name Archie Craig mean anything to you?' he simply smiled and patted her head. I have never forgotten Dr Craig saying to me, 'Jim, I have had to learn a whole new language of love – the language of smiles and touch.' He recalled how as a child he loved when his mother held him, rocked him, stroked his head and straightened his pillow. He believed that just as we were loved into the world, so we ought to be loved out of this world.

Dr Craig came to mind several years after his death when I heard of two men who had been lifelong friends. One was no longer able to speak, the other had great difficulty hearing. Speaking of their continued close relationship, the one who was unable to hear said, 'Some might think our meeting from time to time would be hell for both of us. Though it is certainly not what we would have wanted, yet when we meet we hold hands and a lot of love passes between us.'

❦

Lord Denning was commonly regarded as the finest and most colourful Law Lord of the 20th century. Because he judged each case on its merits, and was willing when necessary to challenge and override legal precedent, he became a very controversial figure in a profession where law was not only built on precedence, but was often like a strait-jacket. Lord Hailsham, when Lord Chancellor, said of Lord Denning, 'The trouble with him is that he is always remaking the law.' Though his judgments were often overruled by the House of Lords, in many cases they later prompted Parliament to change the law. His deep Christian faith was his guide in all he did. Being the last judge to have the right to stay in post for life, he once joked that he had 'every Christian virtue except resignation'! When he finally announced his retirement in 1982, at the age of eighty-three, the satirical magazine *Private Eye* printed a cartoon showing two lawyers reading the headline, 'Denning to Retire'. One of the lawyers was saying to the other, 'I expect the House of Lords will overrule his decision.'

❦

For better or worse friends shape our personalities and outlook. In 1995 I was greatly privileged to spend time in the company of Tom Cousins, a committed churchman and one of America's great philanthropists. Many people and many worthwhile causes have benefited from his great generosity. Tom was the former Chief Executive of Cousins Properties, the firm which built many of Atlanta's most prominent landmarks. Since our first meeting I have been privileged to spend time with Tom and his wife Anne, in Scotland, Atlanta and in the mountains of North Carolina. One evening I shared with Tom the substance of a magazine article I had read about a group of professors at Duke University. When they were asked, 'Who was the guest speaker at your graduation', one professor laughed and said, 'That is not a fair question. That was far too long ago!' A distinguished botanist replied, 'I can remember both events, but not anything that was said.' Tom responded by telling me how he once accepted an invitation to speak at the graduation ceremony of the high school he had attended. He told the graduating students how he had no recollection of who the speaker was when he graduated, or anything he had said. To make sure that would not be true in their case, he had decided to give each of them one share in his company! (Quite a considerable gift.) 'Each year when the annual report arrives you will be helped to remember who your graduation speaker was.' In an address which Tom gave in 2005 to Atlanta's leading citizens, he spoke of his admiration as a young man for the white leaders in their city who had spoken out in support of the civil rights movement. He closed his address with these words, 'I would not presume to suggest how you practise your faith, but the Old and New Testaments, and the Koran, are clear that if we seriously let our faith guide our actions, we would be a better, more fulfilled people, and the world would be a better place. We could again be light to the world, a city set on a hill.'

❦

The eminent conductor Sir Malcolm Sargent was for many years one of the most gifted and attractive personalities in the musical world, a smiling, gifted, compassionate man. He was no stranger to tragedy. While still relatively young he was struck down with TB. Later his daughter Pamela contracted polio and died. Later still he himself contracted cancer. Shortly before his death he took part in a radio 'Any Questions' programme. One of the questions the panel members were asked that night was, 'If three of your wishes could be granted, what would you request?' The answers given by some of the panel members were variations of 'Health, Wealth and Happiness'. But not Sir Malcolm. He said he would not ask for unbroken health for that might rob him of experiences that came through experiencing suffering. 'Sympathy and understanding of others are born in times of one's endurance.' So his first wish would be for sympathy and understanding of others. His second would be for a sense of humour. His third would be for the gift of faith, Christian faith, because he said, 'men and women get from such a faith strength to live and strength to die.'

❧

When Paul McCartney reached the age of 64, he was asked how he felt about writing the song 'When I'm 64', while still a teenager. 'When I dreamed up that song' he said 'I never imagined I would ever be sixty-four and have to face the music.' He went on to tell how he had once met a lady who told him that she was a pianist and that she regularly played this song at their local old folks' home. 'They love it', she said. 'I hope you don't mind but I've had to change the lyrics. I have changed them to "Will you still need me when I'm eighty-four?" Sixty-four is a bit young for most of them.' 'I have no objections at all', said Paul McCartney. 'In fact I like it.'

Saying and Doing Stupid Things

'These haemorrhoids are a real pain in the neck'

Headline in paper: 'Pensioners Wed – Fifty-year friendship ends at altar.'

A daughter tells how her father rang the hospital to confirm that a bed was still available for his operation. When the Sister asked what operation he was due to have, he said, 'A fly-over.' 'Don't you mean a by-pass sir?' said the Sister. 'Oh yes, I knew it had something to do with motorways.'

A few years ago I was invited to be the guest speaker at a district WRI 40th birthday party. I had been asked to give a light-hearted talk on the subject 'Humour – the overlooked sense.' In her introduction, the President said, 'Our only speaker tonight is Dr Simpson. The rest of the evening will be entertainment.' I hope she never realised the full implications of what she had said.

During my year as Moderator, I was invited to speak at a Glasgow dinner. The other speaker was to be Eddie George, the Governor of the Bank of England. That night the chairman introduced me by saying, 'We were all delighted when Dr Simpson was elected Moderator of the Church of Scotland. We were getting awfully tired of these intellectuals.'

A grandmother's advice to her grand-daughter, 'Always be sincere, whether you mean it or not.'

An elderly lady in Chester tells how when BT called to update their records they asked her mother if they could speak to her husband. Suddenly realising that she had never informed BT of her husband's death several years earlier, she said, 'I am sorry he is deceased at the moment.'

A Mrs Matthews, who had wanted all her life to ride on a motor-bike, finally got on one with her nephew and went for a spin. Her 70th birthday being only a few days away, a friend asked her why she did not wait until then, and make it a birthday celebration. 'A 70-year-old woman', she explained, 'would look silly riding a motor-bike.'

The owner of a village shop noticed that a middle-aged gentleman had left his mobile phone on the counter. Scrolling through the saved numbers in the phone he found one entitled 'Mum'. Dialling the number the shop-keeper told the gentleman's mother what had happened. A few minutes later the mobile rang. Before he could say anything, a woman said, 'Martin, you have left your phone in the village shop.'

On returning from a holiday in Germany an elderly couple told their friends how one day they got lost in Cologne. They had carefully noted that they had parked their car on a street named Einbahnstrasse, but when they came to look for it, every street seemed to have the same name. They finally stopped a policeman to ask for help. That is when they learned that Einbahnstrasse means 'One-way street.'

❧

As an old lady stood on the kerb vainly trying to cross a busy city street, a policeman approached her. 'Excuse me, Madam, there is a pedestrian crossing further up the road.' 'Then', retorted the old lady, 'he is having better luck than I am. I have been trying to cross here for the last fifteen minutes.'

❧

An elderly man went to his doctor complaining about a pain in his neck. 'Every time I press my neck, doctor, I get this shooting pain.' The doctor discovered he had two broken fingers.

❧

A restaurant billboard read, *'Daily Specials'*

Monday: Fish 'n' Chips

Tuesday: Fried Chicken

Wednesday: Pork Chops

Thursday: Senior Citizens

Friday: Roast Beef

❦

An American church magazine carried the headline, 'Blind bishop appointed to see.'

Equally confusing was the heading in a local newspaper, 'Patient at death's door – doctors pull him through.'

❦

An old lady predicted bad weather because of all the 'icy bars' on the weather map. Another told her friend that her new sitting room wallpaper had 'a gold pattern embezzled on to it'.

❦

A dear old lady, who had obviously placed the first bet of her life, was at the bookie's window collecting her winnings. Her horse had won and was paid 18 to 1. As the young man handed over her winnings, she said severely, 'I hope this will be a lesson to you.'

❦

A few months before he was due to retire, a doctor said one day to the nurse who worked with him, 'It is a bit embarrassing, but I will need to revise the death certificate I have just given you. Being in too great a hurry, I accidentally signed my name under "Cause of Death".'

❦

An elderly lady said to the air-hostess, 'What a wonderful trip. It was so smooth–just like riding on air.'

A grandmother said to her friend, 'Our family does not have any Christmas traditions. We just do the same thing year after year.'

A Christmas Greetings advert in a newspaper read, 'Adams Undertakers wish to thank all their clients and friends for the support they have received. We are looking forward to being of service to you next year.'

An Eve Belson tells how she was concerned when an elderly couple booked a holiday to Italy through the travel agency in which she worked. They insisted on hiring a car to drive themselves around Rome. Nothing she could say about the frenetic traffic and daredevil Italian drivers could sway them from their plan. The day they came to pick up the tickets and documents, they assured her that she had no reason to worry. They had been to a nearby amusement park, practising their driving techniques on the dodgems!

Several months after her husband's cremation, an elderly friend of his widow, learned that his ashes were still stored in her wardrobe. Expressing her concern about this, she said, 'What if your house burns down?'

An elderly lady finally gave in to her daughter's pleading for her to buy a mobile phone. Shortly after this, her son-in-law received a call from her. The line was so poor that he asked her if the mobile was working OK. She said it was fine, but that the reception was poor because, feeling self-conscious, she had gone into a phone-box to use it.

❧

A few years ago an elderly lady wrote to the BBC, 'What is all this nonsense about that 66-year-old Romanian woman being the world's oldest mother. My mother is 95.'

❧

Two elderly ladies had got off a bus chatting animatedly. They had said their goodbyes and were heading in opposite directions when one called to the other, 'I'll phone you when I get home.' Then on second thoughts she added, 'Better you call me. You will be home before I will.'

❧

A retired maths teacher was discussing with a friend the condition of his old banger. 'It may, like me, be a bit of a wreck, but at least it gets me from x to y.'

❧

An elderly gentleman phoned the electricity supplier to say that his lights had gone out. When asked whether his neighbour's lights were also out, he replied, 'Yes, but a bus has just passed that has its lights on.'

❧

When a minister told an old woman how lovely it was to see her so regularly at the services in the refurbished church, she said, 'It is a joy to come for it is not often I get such a comfortable seat and so little to think about.'

A Rotarian told his friend that his wife had phoned him the previous night from California. 'It was wonderful to hear her voice and realise she was 6,000 miles away.'

When asked by her son-in-law if she had enjoyed the flight back from her holiday, she replied, 'Yes, but for a good part of the journey we had to keep our seat-belts on because of all the flatulence.'

The Ancient World

Wife to retired husband, 'What are you going to do today?'
'Nothing.'
'But you did that yesterday.'
'Yes but I did not finish it.'

The elderly Pope John Paul II made more than than 1,200 pilgrimages outside Italy. In an age of celebrities and politicians who change their priorities according to the latest opinion polls, John Paul II was a man completely without 'spin'. What a wonderful reception he received when he visited Glasgow's Bellahouston Park in 1989. At the close of the open-air Mass the vast crowd began to sing, 'Will ye no come back again.' A priest accompanying the Pope explained that the song the crowd were singing had close associations with Bonnie Prince Charlie. The Pope smiled and said, 'I had afternoon tea with him and his mother yesterday.' The priest was later heard to comment, 'So much for papal infallibility.'

When a new building had to be constructed on Vatican grounds, the architect submitted the plans to Pope John XXIII. A few days later the Pope returned the plans with three Latin words written in the margin: *Non sumus angeli*, meaning 'We are not angels.' The architect could not figure out what the Pope meant until someone pointed out that the plans did not include toilets, a necessity for older men.

Mattie, who had been a widow for several years, died at the age of 99. Not having any family, she had never got round to making a will. Her only relatives were a few great grand-nieces. Not only did they not really know her, not one of them made the effort to attend her funeral. With taxes and other bills to be paid, an auctioneer came to her home. A few strangers also came to view her personal effects. Among the articles to be auctioned was her wedding ring. If someone had said to Mattie when she was alive, 'I love your ring, I will give you $1,000 for it', she would have turned the ring on her finger and said, 'Fifty-six years of marriage and you want to buy this. I would not sell it for 10 million dollars!' The auctioneer's gavel came down, 'Sold. $5.'

❧

The majority of men retire in their mid-sixtics. A few have the financial means to retire earlier, but that option was not open to me. My wife had £50 when I married her. I had not much more. But I have no regrets, for as a wise old Glasgow medical professor once said, 'If you marry a woman for her money, you will very likely pay for every penny of it.'

❧

A Mr Parnell tells how he was driving his mother home through very heavy rain. At one stage they were held up by a motorist who was struggling to push his car to the side of the road. 'That poor man', said his mother. 'Go and give him a hand – it must be dreadful.' When he returned to his car soaked to the skin, his mother sat back with a contented smile on her face. 'I do like to do a good turn whenever I can.'

❧

An American after-dinner speaker was well on in years. He told how he had recently played baseball with his grandsons. Shortly after the game started he made a two-base hit. 'When I got to second base', he said, 'my breath was on first, my heart on third.'

❧

When in the 1960s the film *Battle of Britain* first came out a retired Flight Commander was asked if he was going to see it. 'No I don't think I will bother. I saw the stage show.'

❧

An American couple Jacob (92) and Rebecca (89) were excited about their decision to get married late in life. Jacob, having informed the owner of the local pharmacy that they were getting married, asked him if he sold medication for heart problems and circulation. The reply being in the affirmative, he then asked if he sold medicine for memory problems, arthritis and Alzheimer's. When again informed that they stocked a large variety of such medicines, Jacob inquired about vitamins and medicines for indigestion. Being again informed that they also stocked these, he inquired next whether they sold zimmers, canes and wheel-chairs. On learning that these were among their best-selling lines, Jacob said, 'I wonder then if we could use your store for our wedding present list.'

❧

A hospital admissions clerk tells of a heart-attack victim who, on arrival at the hospital with his wife, was whisked away by the staff. More than an hour passed before his wife was allowed to see him. She was dismayed when she saw him hooked up to elaborate machinery that blipped and hissed and beeped. Tiptoeing toward his bed, she bent over and whispered, 'George, I am here'. Then she kissed him. Suddenly there was a blippety-blip-blip from the heart monitor. Later that day she told a friend. 'After forty-seven years of marriage it was lovely to know I can still make his heart skip a beat when I kiss him.'

❧

Late on in their marriage a husband and wife decided to consolidate their separate bank accounts into one joint account. When he asked her if she understood the paperwork they had just completed, she replied, 'Of course. If I should die before I wake, I pray my spouse my cash to take.'

❧

An elderly couple were touring a historic house where the guide was enthusing about its many charms. 'This house is more than 300 years old and not a post or beam in it has been repaired.' On hearing this the husband turned to his wife and said, 'I am sure we have got the same landlord.'

❧

An Elsbeth Bitzer tells how her grandmother, after a major quarrel with her grandfather, was so angry she refused to speak to him. He had forgotten all about it by the next day, but Grandma went on punishing him with total silence. Finally Grandpa started rummaging through drawers and cupboards. When her grandmother could stand it no longer, she asked impatiently, 'What on earth are you looking for?' 'Thank heavens!' said her grandfather. 'I've found it. Your voice.'

❧

A gentleman who in his retirement had become a keen gardener was puzzled one summer concerning what to do with an over-abundance of courgettes. He finally decided to place some of them on a wooden chair at his garden gate. To the chair he taped a 'Free' sign. When much later in the day he went to the gate, he found the courgettes in a pile on the ground. The chair was, however, gone.

❧

A retired man who had returned with his wife from a four-week golfing trip to Singapore, Thailand and Bali kept waxing eloquent in the club bar about all the wonderful courses they had played. A fellow-member of his local golf-club was overheard quietly saying to the club steward, 'John seems to be suffering from jet-brag.'

❧

Visiting an elderly aunt, her niece was surprised when she answered the door to see her wearing her hat. When her niece inquired if she was just going out, she replied, 'No dear. I always put my hat on when someone comes to the door. If it's someone I really don't want to see, I say I am just going out. But seeing it is you, I've just come in.'

❧

A man tells how one night in a packed cinema he was sitting behind two elderly ladies who were indulging in loud chatter, making it difficult for him to hear the sound-track. Finally he tapped one of them on the shoulder, and said, 'Excuse me. I can't hear!' The reply was not what he expected, 'I should think not. This is a private conversation.'

❦

Just as he was nearing the counter at his local bank a retired gentleman tripped and stumbled forward. Fortunately he did not fall or hurt himself. With a twinkle in his eye the cashier said to him, 'I'm guessing you are here to get your balance.'

❦

For several days Jean's husband had been gently teasing her about her approaching 70th birthday. On the morning of the big day she awoke early and snuggled up to his side. Even she had to chuckle when he opened his eyes wide in mock surprise and said, 'I believe I feel old age creeping up on me.'

❦

My wife is a prolific reader of novels. She would dearly love if libraries had computers which were so programmed that when the ISBN numbers were scanned, the computer would advise, 'You have already read this book.'

❦

A Jane Morrison tells how her father was a GP on a Hebridean island. One day a crofter in his late eighties came to see him with a very painful back. When asked if he had recently undertaken any particularly strenuous activities, the old man at first shook his head, but then he finally remembered. 'I suppose it could have been when I lifted a sack of peat on to my wife's back.'

❧

Dave Allen complained that we spend our lives on the run. We get up by the clock, eat and sleep by the clock, get up again, go to work – and then we retire. And what do they give us? A clock or a watch.

❧

Before making the presentation of a watch to one of his workers who was retiring, the chief executive said, 'As a token of our appreciation, we have created this special gold watch to serve as a reminder of your many years with us. It needs a lot of winding up. It goes slow, and every day it stops working at half-past four.'

❧

As an elderly well-dressed couple passed a beggar sitting on the pavement, he said in a broad Irish accent, 'May the blessin' of the Lord, which brings love, joy, prosperity and all manner of happiness, follow you all the days of your lives.' When the couple walked on without giving him anything, the beggar shouted, 'And never catch up with you.'

❧

A pair of elderly sisters spent their nights reading or sewing. One night as one of them was reading the newspaper, she began mumbling something. Her sister said, 'If you are talking to me would you speak louder? If you are talking to yourself, talk more quietly?'

A retired man who regularly spent hours washing and polishing and tinkering with his car, was dismayed when it had to go into the garage for a few days to have a part replaced. 'Never mind,' consoled his wife, 'the garage may well have visiting hours.'

When our local Perth tennis star George Stewart won the world doubles for the over-85s, he was interviewed on his home court by Scottish television. His tennis friend Ian Strachan, who was in his late seventies, was also interviewed. When Ian was asked how he, a member of the same tennis club, felt about George's achievement, he replied, 'Oh it is a great encouragement to us young folk!'

A Mr Wilson tells how he visited his former neighbour who had moved into an old folks' home. When he arrived he was taken up to his room on the first floor. As he walked down the corridor, he noticed on a large notice-board, a notice which announced: 'Open House Tuesday. Formal – Teeth will be worn.'

After a session with an elderly gentleman who was having many problems with his computer, the technician smiled and said, 'It seems to me the major problem resides between the keyboard and your chair.'

A retired businessman who was on holiday on the Moray coast, asked the professional if there was anyone with whom he could have a game. The professional thought his assistant would be happy to join him. On the first tee the assistant inquired how many strokes he would like. 'Oh', said the man, 'Let us see how it goes without strokes. I play a reasonably good game of golf. My only problem is getting out of deep bunkers.' They came to the 18th all square. For the first time in the round the man buried his second shot in one of the greenside bunkers. Going into the deep bunker with his sand-wedge, he blasted it out to six feet from the pin. After applauding the shot, the assistant said, 'I thought you said you were no good at getting out of bunkers.' 'That is true. Could you possibly give me a hand and help me out of this one.'

An elderly gentleman told how he had become tired pretending he was excited every time it was a contemporary's birthday. What, he asked, is the big deal? 'How often do we have to celebrate that someone was born? All you have done is not die for twelve months. Is that such a big accomplishment?'

Laughing at Ourselves

You don't stop laughing because you grow old.
You grow old because you stop laughing.

When old folk make jokes about their infirmities, mistakes and forgetfulness, it is a clear indication they are coping well. One woman writes, 'Concerned that my body was so out of shape, I got my doctor's permission to join a fitness club and start exercising. I decided to take an aerobics class for seniors. I bent, twisted, gyrated, jumped up and down and perspired for half-an-hour. But by the time I got my leotard on, the class was over.'

❧

A frail but cheery old man told how every day he has close contact with six other gentlemen. As soon as he wakes up WILL POWER helps him out of bed. Then he visits JOHNNY LOO. When CHARLIE CRAMP visits him, he takes up a lot of his attention. At other times ARTHUR RITIS shows up and stays around all day. Each night before going to bed he spends ten minutes with JOHNNY WALKER.

❧

Jack Parr said, 'Looking back my life seems like one obstacle race, with me as its chief obstacle.'

❧

A delightful retired businessman said of himself 'I am 42 round the chest, 52 round the waist, 102 round the golf course, and a nuisance round the house.'

❧

A lady, who felt she needed some new clothes, spent an evening poring over mail-order catalogues. Finally she put them aside saying, 'It is no use. My body is out of fashion.'

❧

A speaker at a dinner at which I was present began by drawing attention to his big ears, little hair and a body really too short for his legs. He then went on to tell his audience that he had been even less handsome as a boy. 'In fact the first time I ever played Hide and Seek, no one came looking for me.' That touch of self-deprecating humour endeared him to his audience.

❧

When an octogenarian complained to his doctor of a sore right knee, the doctor told him he really could not expect to have painless knees at his age. 'But doctor', he said, 'my left knee is also 83, and it does not hurt.'

❧

An elderly gentleman who had just celebrated his 55th wedding anniversary was asked, 'Are there any secrets between you two? Do you ever hide anything from each other?' 'Well, yes,' replied the old man with a sly smile. 'I have £1,000 in a bank that Mary does not know about. And she has £1,000 in a bank that I don't know about.'

❧

One winter's day a pensioner was heard to say, 'One of the benefits of dull winter days is that I don't lose my sun glasses. The best thing about warm summer days is that I don't lose one glove.' Another was overheard telling her friend that she had only two teeth left – one in the top and one in the bottom. 'I am so grateful' she said, 'that they hit.'

The elderly Andrew Carnegie would occasionally enjoy mixing with throngs of ordinary folk in busy streets. A friend tells how they were travelling together one day in a tramcar in Princes Street in Edinburgh, when the conductor came to collect fares. Andrew gave him half-a-crown – a very considerable sum of money a hundred years ago, and told him to keep the change. The conductor gasped in astonishment. 'Are you mad, or are you Carnegie?' 'I might be both' said the multi-millionaire. Andrew and his friend laughed heartily. Nobody on the bus recognised him.

A Senior's Prayer

(Anonymous)

Today, dear Lord I'm 80 – there's much I've left undone
So I hope that you will let me live, till I am 81.
But then if I haven't finished everything I want to do
Would you let me stay a little while – until I'm 82?

There are so many places I want to go, so much yet to see;
Do you think you could manage to make it 83?
The world is changing very fast, and so much yet in store
It would be nice to be around and live to be 84!

And then, and then, if by your grace, I'm allowed to stay alive,
Couldn't you stretch a little point and make it 85?
All the wonderful changes in your world make me want to stick
And just see what might happen, if I live to be 86.

I know Lord that I'm pushing it, and there'll be fun in heaven –
But if you need the room up there, I'll wait till I'm 87.
I know by then I might be frail, and my memory in a state,
But I'd try not to be a nuisance and still useful at 88!

By then I'll have seen many things and had a super time,
And quite ready to leave if you call me home at 89.
But maybe by then you'll be ready, to smile and let me go,
And with my friends to party at the big 9-0.

Facing the Final Curtain

In spite of all the advances of modern medicine, the mortality rate remains 100%! Yet our culture does not encourage us to think about dying until we are about to die.

Though everyone knows they are going to die, yet for the major part of their lives, few really believe it or talk about it. Not knowing what to say about the last earthly act, many say nothing.

Woody Allen said, 'I'm not afraid of death, but I'd rather be somewhere else when it happens.' Dying has seldom been popular, perhaps because it is not good for the complexion! In an interview on his 78th birthday, Andrew Carnegie said, 'I have passed another milestone and I am not keen on going ahead too fast. This earth of ours is such a heaven to me that I want to stay here just as long as I can.' Society is organised on the assumption that most people, like Carnegie, want to go on living, and will do almost anything rather than die. One night when I was driving home and seeing cars coming towards me, it suddenly struck me that all that separated me from the oncoming drivers was a thin white line. Yet because of my strong belief that these other drivers did not want to die any more than I did, I was not afraid that one of them might suddenly decide to cross over to my side of the road.

When a doctor said to an elderly gentleman, 'I'm not a magician, I cannot make you young again.' The patient retorted, 'I don't want you to. All I want is to go on getting older.' Most people would agree with his sentiment, but not everyone. The historian A. J. P. Taylor said, 'The greatest problem about old age is that it may go on too long.' That was the fear expressed so powerfully by Sir Terry Pratchett in his Richard Dimbleby Lecture, entitled, 'Assisted Death'. He spoke of the fear of increasing feebleness, and the progressive loss of our physical and mental powers. For others the great fear is the loneliness of old age. When, because of a crippling terminal illness, old folk do not want to 'exist' any longer, it is often said that their minds are disturbed. Sir Terry wondered whether in some cases, their minds were in fact better balanced. They do not want, he said, to have a long uncomfortable wait in 'God's Waiting Room.'

❧

Death is part of our finitude. In his book, *Meanings of Death and Life*, William Hocking reminds us that death spares us endless frailty. 'Just think of the monstrous picture of life in which the older generation does not pass away. Plato would still be writing dialogues while David Hume would still be refuting them.' I thank God that we do not live to the reputed age of Methuselah. I thank God that we old-timers do not go on weighing down the human race with our conservatisms and prejudices, and with costly medical care.

❧

The crucial support and tender loving care provided by hospice staff and volunteers to those whose bodies are too broken to mend any more, never ceases to amaze me. Though the law of averages might suggest that somewhere, at some time, a hospice must have messed up, I have yet to hear of it. Nothing seems to be of too much trouble to hospice staff – always someone to listen, to give a hug, to sit and hold a hand, always someone there for the family as well. Even though the emphasis in the hospices and Maggie Centres which I have visited is not so much on dying as living, yet as a result of the hospice movement conversation is more open between loved ones about death. Stories of triumphant dying are numerous. But I wonder, is there a danger the pendulum will go too far? Someone recently sought to collect the 'last words' of notable people. Now though it may be inspiring to read these last words, I would not want the pressure of having to come up with an outstanding one-liner with my dying breath. Imagine, if after hours of fretting trying to decide what would be the final sentence I would utter, I was to forget the wording! I recall my own brother's death while he was still in his forties. As I sat by his hospital bed-side, listening intently, he said, 'Jim, I love you.' That is more than enough for me.

❧

William Sloan Coffin was the chaplain to Yale University before becoming the minister of the Riverside Church in Manhattan. He spent his life raging against bigotry, injustice, the Vietnam War, nuclear arms and homophobia. In the mid-1980s his son was tragically drowned in Boston harbour as a result of a car accident. Ten days after his son's death he spoke these profound words to his congregation: 'Nothing so infuriates me as the incapacity of seemingly intelligent people to get it through their heads that God doesn't go around this world with his fingers on triggers, his fist around knives, his hands on steering wheels. God is against all unnatural deaths. Jesus spent an inordinate amount of time delivering people from paralysis, insanity, leprosy and muteness... The one thing that should never be said when someone dies is, "It is the will of God." Never do we know enough to say that. My consolation lies in knowing that it was not the will of God that Alex die, that when the waves closed over that sinking car, God's was the first of our hearts to break.'

Many years later in an interview which Dr Coffin gave shortly before his own death, he spoke of how he intended to cooperate gracefully with the inevitable, to die gently, without fuss, without fury. He spoke of his shortness of breath even before he got out of bed in the morning, of how his tennis-player legs were long gone, of how though he could still with difficulty walk slowly around the house he needed a wheelchair to leave it. Then he added, 'But I have really nothing to complain about. Very fortunately I have not lost my marbles.' He spoke of the joy and satisfaction of having a new book published, *Credo*, which had rapidly climbed the best-seller lists. In the final chapter of that book entitled 'The end of life' he writes, 'The only way to have a good death is to lead a good life. Lead a good one, full of curiosity, generosity and compassion, and there is no need at the close of the day to rage against the dying of the light. We can go gentle into that good night.' In his eighties, Lyman Abbot penned similar thoughts, 'I enjoy my home, my friends, my life. I shall be sorry to part from them. But I have always stood in the bow looking forward with hopeful anticipation. When the time comes for me to put out to sea, I think I shall be standing in the bow and looking forward with eager interest and glad hopefulness to the new world to which the unknown voyage will take me.' I hope I will too.

❦

On old Roman tombstones there sometimes appeared the letters NFFNSNC. The Latin words for which these letters stood were so well known that only the initials were needed. Unlike SAGA which few people know stands for Social Amenity and Golden Age, the Romans knew these letters stood for *Non fui, fui, non sum, non curo* – I was not, I was, I am not, I do not care. For most of us to speak thus of life and death would be dishonest. We do care. It does matter whether death is the end, or whether it is an open door to an eternal morning. Especially is this true when the death of a loved one occupies our thoughts.

❦

Recalling his first parish, Professor Reinhold Niebuhr, one of the outstanding church ministers and thinkers of the 20th century, wrote,

'Two old ladies were dying shortly after I assumed responsibility for the parish. They were both equally loyal members of the congregation. But I soon noted that their manner of facing death was strikingly dissimilar. One old lady was too pre-occupied with self, too aggrieved that Providence should not have taken account of her virtue in failing to protect her from this grievous illness, to be able to face death with any serenity... The other lady had brought up a healthy and wholesome family, though her husband was subject to periodic fits of insanity, which forced her to be the bread-winner as well as the home-maker. Just as her two splendid daughters had finished their training and were eager to give their mother a secure and quiet evening of life, she was found to be suffering from cancer. I stood weakly at her bedside while she told me what passages of scripture to read to her, most of which expressed gratitude for all the mercies she had received in life. She was particularly grateful for her two daughters and their love; and she faced death with the utmost peace of soul.'

❦

Dr Harry Fosdick in one of his many books devotes a section to death. He asks us to imagine two unborn babies in a mother's womb, conversing about the prospect that lies ahead of them. One says, 'Leaving this womb can mean nothing but death. We are absolutely dependent on this matrix which sustains and feed us.' Says the other, 'But nature has been developing us for nine months. Nature is not utterly irrational. She is preparing us for something.' Answers the unbelieving babe, 'Describe then if you can the kind of world you think we are going to be born into. What is it like?' That of course would completely stump the believing babe. 'I cannot describe it,' he replies. 'I have no idea what it is like. But I am sure nature would never do what she has been doing all these months with no meaning or purpose in the process.' To which the unbelieving babe answers with scorn, 'That is blind faith.' But the believing babe was right.

❦

Sheep dogs are very much part of Highland life. During lambing season they will often finish the day exhausted, but not a single sheep will have been lost. A poetic Highland preacher once elaborated on this fact. 'The Lord is my shepherd. Aye and more than that he has two collie dogs, named Goodness and Mercy. With the shepherd going before, and them behind, even poor sinners like you and me can hope to win home at the last.'

❧

Though the very fine doctor in A. J. Cronin's novel, *The Keys of the Kingdom* is an agnostic, he is one of the first to volunteer to go to China to help fight a plague that is raging there. Some time later, as he himself lies dying from the plague, he confesses to the priest by his bedside that he still cannot believe in God. To which the priest tenderly replies, 'Perhaps not my son, but he certainly believes in you.' I have known many agnostics of whom I would have said the same.

❧

My faith is strong that the love of God which has been such a blessing throughout my life will not forsake me when the final curtain falls. I have lived the dream. I have enjoyed being busy, and hopefully of some use. I continue to enjoy summer, winter, autumn and spring. Should life suddenly withdraw her favours, I hope I will ever be mindful that for many years the sun has shone on my back. I hope I will continue to walk the world with gratitude. I hope what years remain will continue to be creative ones. If I could ask a favour of God it would be that the curtain might fall for me, before it does for my wife – I would be lost without her – and before I become a nuisance to my family or no longer able to recognise them or respond to them and my surroundings. It would be a real bonus if I could shake hands with death with my mental faculties intact. Another problem I have with death has to do with those who will be left behind. When that day comes I suspect my family and those friends who have become part of the fabric of my life, will shed a few tears. When the final curtain falls I will feel more for them than for myself.

A Final Laugh

Old card players never die; they just shuffle off.

Old florists never die – they make other arrangements.

Old psychologists never die; they are forever Jung.

Old comedians never die – the just go to old jokes homes.

Old bacteriologists never die – they just go out to Pasteur.

A number of people were miffed when after 21 years as minister of Dornoch Cathedral I intimated that I would be leaving the Cathedral to take up a trouble-shooting role for the national church. I recall one elderly member saying to me, 'One of the reasons I joined the Cathedral was that I hoped you would one day conduct my funeral service. Now I hear you won't be able to do it.' 'Margaret', I said, 'I will be more than happy to conduct your funeral. All you have to do is to die within the next month!' That did not however appeal to her!

❧

One day an elderly gentleman met in the street, a man he had not seen for some time. When he was younger he had known the man and his brother well. Puzzled as to which of the two brothers it was, he said, 'Was it you or your brother who died?'

❧

The British novelist and poet Walter de la Mare suffered a severe illness. For some time his life was in the balance. His daughter asked him one day if there was anything she could bring him – fruit or flowers. 'No', said the poet weakly, 'too late for fruit, too soon for flowers.'

A thrifty Scotsman, proud of his lifelong prudence, was on his deathbed. His family had gathered round to share his final moments. When he inquired where his wife was, Jean, taking his hand replied, 'I'm here my darling.' He then asked where his son and daughter were. 'We are here too, Dad.' 'OK,' said the old man, 'If you are all here, why is the light on in the kitchen?'

The mother of Zsa Zsa Gabor was still having cosmetic surgery in her 90s. Before going under the knife she instructed the surgeon to complete the procedure even if she died on the operating table!

Just before the funeral service of her husband, the undertaker asked her how old her husband was. 'Ninety-eight', she replied, 'two years older than me.' When the undertaker said, 'So you are ninety-six', she replied, 'Hardly worth going home, is it?'

A father who died left his prize collection of clocks to his son. The son spent the rest of his life winding up the estate!

Often at family weddings, elderly aunts would say to their nephew John, who was a handsome young man, 'It will be your turn next.' John tells how he was once tempted at a family funeral to say to one these aunts, 'It will be your turn next,' but he refrained!

❧

A man tells how one day after he was widowed, he began thinking about his own mortality. When later that day his daughter phoned, he told her that he felt it was time for them to talk about where he would like to be buried. There was a pause at the other end of the phone. Finally she said, 'Wait a second, did you say "married" or "buried"?' When he repeated 'buried', she said, 'Oh OK, fine.'

❧

A tombstone in Los Angeles bears the following inscription: Helen Schultz – A special person who is fondly remembered as a devoted wife, mother, grandmother, friend, and for correcting everyone's grammar. Does she 'lay' here or 'lie' here?

❧

A Mr Marr tells how during an interview for a job in his firm, he asked one applicant a philosophical question in the hope of gaining insight into her personality. 'If you could spend an evening conversing with any person, alive or dead, whom would you choose?' With enthusiasm she replied, 'The living one.'